AND SHE DANCED BY THE LIGHT OF THE MOON

Catherine Nadal

AuthorHouse™
1663 Liberty Drive
Bloomington, IN 47403
www.authorhouse.com
Phone: 833-262-8899

Some of the names of people and places mentioned in this book have been changed. Others, however, gave permission to use their names or are now deceased and living in the afterlife.

This book is printed on acid-free paper.

ISBN: 978-1-6655-7456-3 (sc)
ISBN: 978-1-6655-7464-8 (hc)
ISBN: 978-1-6655-7457-0 (e)

Library of Congress Control Number: 2022920265

Print information available on the last page.

Published by AuthorHouse 11/22/2022

authorHOUSE®

AND SHE DANCED BY THE LIGHT OF THE MOON

This book is dedicated to those who have filled my life with love, music and laughter living here and in the afterlife.

FOREWORD

By Dr. Laurie Nadel

"When travel is made to be too easy and comfortable,

its spiritual meaning is lost." -- Rumi

She has traveled many roads, seen and unseen. Her journeys have taken her to the heart of war and into the mystical corridors of a spiritualist college overseas. A colonel in the US Army Reserve who served as a nurse in Iraq, Catherine Nadal has a dual career as a respected medium. Born with the gift of seeing into the nonphysical realm of Spirit, she has been tested and recognized by the Forever Family Foundation as a respected medium.

Although these two careers may seem incompatible, she explains how she does both in her breakthrough memoir

And She Danced by the Light of the Moon. Her military career has contributed to a positive and pragmatic mindset. "*The military teaches you to expect the unexpected,*" she writes. "*One of the biggest lessons I learned in the military was to always be prepared.*"

Preparing to enter the Unknown necessitates shifting attention away from the five physical senses to the sixth sense, that part of us that knows without the conscious use of reasoning. Intuitive knowing is, by its nature, spontaneous and nonlinear. Shifting the focus of attention from the external world of people activities and things to the inner world of impressions, sounds, sensations, and images that can be verified but not quantified requires years of study, apprenticeship, training, and practice. Catherine invites the reader along with her on these voyages of exploration.

As Rumi observed in the 13th century, complex and difficult journeys open the way for spiritual growth. Living through the extremes of war punctuated by the need for quietude that her soul path requires focus, discipline, integrity, and a commitment to service for the greater good. As the author observes in these pages, her military and nursing background also served to strengthen her skills as a psychic and medium.

As a psychic whose talent for reading coffee grounds will draw an instant crowd in a café or restaurant, Cathy's intuitive foresight has proven accurate for hundreds of her clients.

As a medium, she receives and transmits facts and details that are private and personal, known only to the person receiving the reading and the entity who is communicating. As she explains in these pages, Catherine can receive a deceased person's name, physical description, and even facts about an object, a pet or a conversation that occurred between the spirit and the sitter. A member of the Forever Family Foundation, her purpose in writing this book goes beyond providing evidence of the afterlife. The intention of the Foundation is to offer healing to souls in distress. She writes,

"Our work as mediums is based on providing support and guidance through messages of evidence of spirit to loved ones during the grief process."

Whether you are sitting with her for a reading or being absorbed by the stories she shares in these pages, you can't help feeling uplifted by Cathy Nadal's intuitive sparkle, warmth, and empathy.

It has been my privilege to get to know her in person, thanks to *Coast-to-Coast AM with George Noory.* For more than 30 years, Coast-to-Coast AM has been the premier talk radio show devoted to exploring the unknown, expecting the unexpected and discovering new information about mind, body and spirit. Through the magic of synchronicity, Catherine woke up in the middle of the night and heard me talking to George about the role of intuition in healing. Our last names are almost identical—Nadal and Nadel. Thinking that my name was Nadal, like hers, Catherine reached me through my website. When we discovered that our last names were separated by an "a" and an "e" we couldn't help laughing. Although I have not been in the military, in my first career as a journalist, I was a reporter for *Newsweek* in a war zone. After twenty years in journalism, I went to graduate school to become a psychologist and have spent the last thirty years helping people whose lives were shattered by disasters, including veterans and first responders. Curiouser and curiouser, my first book made intuition mainstream after two appearances on *Oprah. Sixth Sense: Unlocking*

Your Ultimate Mind Power included interviews with Vietnam veterans, police officers and dozens of others who owed their survival to trusting their hunches under fire.

We share an archetype, the Explorer. An archetype is a soul blueprint that Carl Jung has identified as a driving force in the psyche. As our friendship grows, so does my respect for Catherine's knowledge, experience, and worldview that encompasses those unseen places where consciousness exists beyond time and space.

Whether you believe in the existence of an afterlife or not, I invite you to turn the page and let Catherine be your guide. Her warmth, humor, integrity and common sense comes through every page.

Let the adventure begin…

Dr. Laurie Nadel has had a dual career in psychology and journalism. The author of seven books including *The Five Gifts: Discovering Hope Healing and Strength When Disaster Strikes* and the four-time best-seller *Sixth Sense: Unlocking Your Ultimate Mind Power,* she has written for *The New York Times,* CBS News and other major news organizations.

www.laurienadel.com

Preface

This book offers my personal recollections of events that have changed my life and set me on the path of discovering my lifework as a psychic medium. The events unfold and illuminate the hardships, doubt, and precognition amid the unknown from my childhood to a combat zone and beyond. In looking back on a life well-lived, I find no prouder memories than those I have shared with others in learning the many hard lessons in life and being dedicated to helping those understand grief and the afterlife.

As a small child, my sister and I followed the neighborhood kid Brian up the long driveway to see the Mitchell Mansion. We lived on Mitchell Avenue in Yonkers, New York; this area is known as the Bryn Mawr section of Yonkers. In 1978, the Mitchell Mansion stood in the middle of our block and was a very impressive stately home. Brian told us he would take us inside, as it had been abandoned for many years and was well-known in the history of Yonkers. We thought he wanted to scare us, and we were right.

As we stepped in, I immediately looked up at the huge staircase. There was a window at the top where the sunshine poured through, making everything glisten. Looking down, Brian pointed out a few items that were scattered on the floor. One item was an old-fashioned tuxedo tie.

"Look," he said. "That must have been old man Mitchell's tie." Then he followed it up with, "Are you scared yet?"

I remember looking up at Brian and his squinty eyes, saying quickly, "No, I like it here."

He seemed annoyed and a little bit creeped out, so he walked us out to the very overgrown backyard with its large, old fruit trees. Brian mumbled on about this area being all farmlands at one point, and the three of us just stood there staring at the weeds. Although the weeds were above our knees, to me, it was just beautiful. The grounds seemed to vibrate with history and echo a ghostlike presence. Perhaps I was the only one who could feel it.

Well, that was it, the big reveal of the mansion, courtesy of our neighbor Brian. I never entered the home again, but that quick visit unlocked my young heart and eyes to the psychic gift that lived inside me. In 1980, the mansion was demolished, and a cul-de-sac of homes was built in its place. Thinking back to the Mitchell Mansion, this may have been the beginning of my relationship with the spirit world and my continued quest to understand more.

Introduction

Catherine Nadal has lived a different life than most. Gifted with psychic abilities as a child, she felt lost without direction. What she did not know at that time was that realizing her true identity would take time and patience.

In a fascinating retelling of her personal recollections, Nadal shares insight into the events that changed her life and set her on the path to discover her lifework as a psychic medium. She illuminates the hardships, doubts, and premonitions that occurred in her childhood, in combat, and beyond. She also reveals how she found direction while on a journey wrapped in self-discovery, mystery, and courage that eventually led her to help others understand grief and the afterlife. Throughout her story, Nadal reminds us that it's never too late to change our conversations or paths, to keep discovering the unknown, and express gratitude for the gifts that life places along the way.

And She Danced by the Light of the Moon chronicles the experiences and insights of a psychic medium as she reveals how she discovered her lifework and purpose.

Contents

Chapter 1 1
Chapter 2 7
Chapter 3 14
Chapter 4 20
Chapter 5 36
Chapter 6 50
Chapter 7 55
Chapter 8 61
Chapter 9 74
Chapter 10 80
Chapter 11 84

Chapter 1

"What a long, strange trip it's been" is a well-known compilation album title by the Grateful Dead that features the great song "Truckin'." I have often thought of this album title from time to time in my life. Just when I think I have figured it out or honestly believe I understand life, I am left surprised. *Unique* and *unusual* would be good adjectives to explain my life so far, I might say. Just the other day, I found myself retelling a story of long ago—something that happened to me that completely changed my life. As I was sharing this experience, I realized my journey was filled with creativity, and the people, places, and events each somehow changed my life. The story I was telling someone led me all the way back to when I was in my senior year in high school.

It was an autumn day that I found out through a friend about this "new age witch shop" called Enchantments in New York City. My friend was a few years older than me, and she was always filling me in on distinct parts of her life. On this day, she was showing off her newest tattoo, and we started to talk about the symbols of the artwork. Her tattoo was a beautiful crescent moon with stars set in a misty sky. Our conversation, like always, led into music and lyrics. We started to talk about Fleetwood Mac and Stevie Nicks, and my friend mentioned the shop.

She described the Enchantments shop as like the velvet underground that Stevie Nicks sang about in the song "Gypsy." Over the years, locals in the San Francisco area have identified this place as a hole-in-the-wall clothing shop. Stevie Nicks has mentioned to her fans that The Velvet Underground was where she had found different items to piece together to create her '70s gypsy-styled wardrobe. She sings about revisiting the gypsy of her past as she realizes the gypsy who has remained years later. This lyrical concept ignites the idea that Stevie Nicks has always stayed true to herself. My friend mentioned that she had only been to the witch shop Enchantments once, but as she described it, I knew I needed to experience it. My friend was glowing as she still had the magic of the experience with her. I just knew this was a place I needed to visit, so I set off to find Enchantments in New York City to discover that exact same magic. From that day forward, magic has never left my life.

It was late in the afternoon on a day in 1986 when I first stepped into Enchantments on East Ninth Street between First and Second Avenue. The tiny iconic witch shop with books, spells, and cats instantly appealed to me. Standing there watching the customers and staff, I was fascinated with the *at-home* feeling I had. One of the employees struck up a conversation with me about essential oils, mentioning without hesitation that I should take home the pure scent of gardenia. Shocked and haunted, I agreed; this was my mother's favorite scent and was the same strong smell of the flowers in her wedding bouquet. It was that strong odor that almost caused her to almost faint at the altar, as she often retold the story. On the train home, with the gardenia oil in my purse, I was in deep thought about how this employee knew to select the oil and the oddity of the meaning. I believed she sensed my mother around me in spirit, I thought as I looked out the window of the Metro-North train. My mother died suddenly in 1985, when I was only sixteen.

Everyone lives his or her own life, no matter how some people feel forced in any one direction. In my teens, things started to happen to me which set me on a course of events of change and excitement. Reflecting now, many years later, these events occurred in my life and helped define who I am today. Perhaps as you are reading this, you are also reflecting on the events that occurred throughout your life that set you on your path. In your reflection, maybe you will find some of the events that still surprise you to this day.

There was no way my father would have it any other way: his two daughters would attend a Roman Catholic, all-girls high school in Westchester County. My father was a devoted Catholic and proud third-degree Knight of Columbus. He believed in God and enjoyed his parish. Without further discussion, my sister and I enrolled. I had voiced my opinion that I wanted to attend a local public school that I could walk to in the neighborhood. My father would not entertain that conversation. At the time, I did not consider myself a strong Catholic. I knew what I was taught, but struggled with the validity of the stories of the Bible.

When I was fourteen and starting high school, my father thought it would be an enlightening experience for my sister and me to attend a Catholic Youth Organization (CYO) weekend for teens. I was not looking forward to this enlightening experience, but we did attend. I knew I was reluctant because it felt forced and was not my idea of fun. I guess I should not be amazed that I got in trouble for socializing with the teens and not taking the weekend seriously. According to the weekend counselors, we were there to discover and learn.

My first lesson hit me on that first evening, after being dropped off by my father. The lesson was about the impact of the word "influence." The camp leaders influenced the teens with Bible scripture to show them the way in life. Some of the teens I encountered were not influenced at all, and had been sent there because they had been "bad" influences. One girl and I were in almost in a fistfight, after she pulled the pillow out from under my head. The staff had forced my sister and me to be roommates with her. A few of the guys hinted at being under the influence or being there for being bad influences, and we believed them. The entire experience was not enlightening at all. I knew my father sent us there since my mother struggled severely with alcohol addiction. Dad relied heavily on his faith and often spoke about love and forgiveness. I did not need to learn the lesson of forgiveness. I had already forgiven her. This was not the enlightening experience I needed; I felt like something was missing in my life. I truly knew I needed to find my tribe, and these teens at CYO camp were not my tribe.

This CYO camp was beautifully nestled in the deep woods in a very peaceful setting. The place had a real seventies vibe and seemed to be very outdated. Almost everyone thought the place had a positive reputation. I wondered why I needed to attend this place; perhaps I needed to realize how miserable a person could feel at fourteen. Two of the most reoccurring questions asked by the staff were, "Where are you headed?" and "Where do you want to go?" These questions were based on spirituality and growth of faith. In my mind, I felt it could only mean my career; that was why I was attending high school, I thought. I was not headed anywhere. At that age, I felt powerless because I was a teenager.

Back at high school, the staff announced we could become nurses' aides at the convent to make money; I signed up. I knew instantly this was my best bet for paid work, and my father would approve. The convent experience carved out discipline for me in a unique way. I had discipline, but this experience was for me to "watch discipline, understand it, and respect it." The nuns knew it, lived it, and loved it. The concept of joining something that you understood and were proud of was appealing to me. I understood this concept, and now I know why I was able to join the military and work with senior leaders for thirty years: because of the discipline the nuns taught me. They had a mother superior; the military had a general and more generals. They had vows; we had taken oaths. They had uniforms, and we had uniforms. The nuns believed in their mission, and we believed in ours. Throughout my later high school years, while working at the convent, I started to realize I wanted a different life. I knew I was brave and courageous, and I wanted to find adventure. Reflecting on that time, the people I found, especially the nuns, made me feel like I belonged. However, in my heart, I just did not understand why.

Sometimes in life, you do not know where you are headed, but you want to go forward anyway. This is how I felt during my entire teenage years: not knowing where I was headed, but eager to see where the road ahead would lead. From an early age, I learned about disappointment. Living with my mother, who struggled with an alcohol addiction, led me to learn to accept disappointment, broken promises, and changes of plans. Part of my driven determination in life and in my career has been to conquer and control the path of life and push it in the direction I wanted it to go. Life can be easy or hard. "It is your choice," my father used to tell me, and he was completely correct. To this day, I can hear him say these words, with an additional sentence about remembering to "use your brain."

Do you believe in chance? Do you believe in things that are meant to be? These were questions I often found myself reviewing during my teens. As events unfolded, I pondered those questions even more. If you had a choice, or were given a choice, would you select the same life? Every teen struggles with growing pains, and I struggled thinking I was not unique, pretty, or cool enough. All I knew is what I did not want to be: a disappointment. I found myself lost in music a lot, especially listening to Journey. The lyrics still bring me back to those days of decision-making. *Rolling Stone* magazine kept me updated on the music scene as I was daydreaming in Yonkers of a life I did not have.

How many people really get to know you in life? As a teenager, you honestly believe that everyone knows you, but that could not be farther from the truth. Sure, your parents might have a hint of what you like, and your closest friends might guess what you do not like. Yet, who do they really know? Teenagers build the people they hope to be. Perhaps some are building it in midflight, but the building takes time. Many teens go through this time unaware of the statements, actions, and dreams that form them. Most of us children of the eighties expressed ourselves through our hair, makeup, and clothing. We were blessed to be living in the material world that Madonna often belted out over the radio waves. I was no different, yet I tended to lean toward the heavy metal and rock side of the music world. Nevertheless, I still saw life through the same mirror as the rest of them.

I often think of the high school mixers—yes, there were coed dances between the Catholic high schools. Walking into the schools and onto the gymnasium dance floors felt electric. They often had strobe lights and hanging glittery decorations, just like a movie set from a teen horror flick. Nonetheless, the idea of a mixer dance was always exciting just to see who would show up. The music was perfect, typical eighties stuff, and we all looked like we had been dropped into a shopping mall. Many of the kids were eager to find true love while the rest of us were checking out the fashion and the total scene. The actual idea of meeting anyone there never felt believable to me among the loud music and crowded dance floor.

In Yonkers, we had this great record store called Sam Goody's where I spent a lot of time and money. The album covers told part of a story to me, and the lyrics on the inside record jacket told the rest. Music was my constant friend. Everyone relates to his or her first something. My first kiss was in my basement with my CYO boyfriend while the Pretenders' song "Back on the Chain Gang" played in the background. Many years later, I met that first boyfriend when I was living in New York City. He was bragging about his stint in prison and a brief story in the *NY Post* that featured his arrest.

As he stood in front of me, the lyrics of that Pretenders song rolled around in my mind, especially the line, "I found a picture of you, o-o-oh, o-o-oh, / Those were the happiest days of my life." You see, as teenagers, we never seem to understand how the universe creatively works. Young hearts do not understand why some relationships never really take off from the start. Adults and parents often guide teens in their times of heartbreak; however, teens never understand the unknown question of why. Years later, I truly knew why the CYO boyfriend and I were not meant to be.

We are building ourselves in flight, as I said earlier. When meeting others, it was always about the other person. I found a creative way to somehow get others to reveal themselves to me. On several occasions, I was stunned by how truly fascinating others can be and sadly found how phony some truly are.

In my first year at high school, my English teacher, an elderly nun, gave the class a public speaking assignment. She stated she wanted all the assignments to be original, creative, and educational. Furthermore, she wanted the public speaking to include a demonstration. After class, I asked her if she would approve my topic of tobacco. She asked me to give her my outline. When she realized I would cover the history of tobacco as well as its effects, she seemed fascinated. She told me that she approved of it. She wanted me to know that she felt it was daring and different, and she trusted me. The moment I heard her use the word "trust," a concept I struggled with as a child, I was instantly motivated. The following week, I stood before my fellow classmates and delivered my speech on tobacco with a follow-up demonstration on hand-rolling a cigarette. The experience was enlightening to the students. First, many of the students did not know the history of tobacco, and many of them were shocked that my topic was even approved. I received a remarkably high grade for that public speaking assignment; the nun expressed how creative and detailed my talk was. In my mind, I believed she was just pleased that no one lit up the hand-rolled cigarettes. From that day on, my first-year classmates looked at me in a slightly unusual way, and I looked back at them with a feeling of being original.

During your teenage years, you can see some of your future, but only if you are paying close attention to it. I wandered around a lot as a teen, often with neighborhood kids, discovering the mall and the golf course, and finding old train tracks. It was all part of the journey. Bits and pieces of life often came together in our minds on those journeys. We all came from different homes, with different stresses, and none of us was in the same situation. The concept of time is always either on or off your mind as a teen. We would often tell ourselves we could do it later until that later was waiting until the last minute, and we were out of time. Now as adults, we seek for getting more time to complete almost everything. Much of these journeys with the neighborhood kids taught me to listen—truly listen. When the talkative are instantly quiet or when you can only hear yourself breathe and the birds chirp, someone is deep in thought. Chances are, it might just be you.

Chapter 2

Sophomore year for me was unique; I was finally getting the hang of the courses at school and learning my nursing skills at the convent. I genuinely enjoyed walking into the neighboring town of Bronxville, doing some shopping, and just being alone. At fifteen, I was pretty absorbed with myself, like many teens usually are, but one day seemed to change my outlook on life.

As I entered the town, a speedy little sports car whizzed by, blasting the familiar song "Hotel California" by the Eagles. My head swung in the same direction to catch a glimpse, but it was almost gone down the narrow street. Something about that split-second vision left me almost tingling. During my store shopping, the song lyrics came to mind, especially the line "and I was thinking to myself this could be heaven or this could be hell." This phrase was fitting to the time and place I was experiencing in my mind. At that age, I should have been happy and thrilled to be living life. However, I was dealing with the constant stress of a severely damaged alcoholic mother at home. My heaven, my hell—and this was my life, I thought, as I started back walking home carrying my small bag of cosmetics.

Within a week, I was stepping out of the card shop in Bronxville, and there was the loud sound of that same sports car's motor. I looked up, and it pulled into a parking spot. This young man with long hair stepped out and smiled across at me. I froze. This was the "Hotel California" car, I thought, and there were those tingles again. I threw my hand up to a half-wave and hurried down the sidewalk, trying to mix into the pedestrian traffic. He was walking across the street on the opposite sidewalk. As I turned back, I noticed he was still smiling. I bolted into a store. Once inside the store, I felt safe. I instantly thought to myself, *This is so stupid. Am I hiding from a stranger?*

Once I thought it out and assumed he was just a friendly person, I walked out the sliding doors. Outside, I saw him leaning against the parking meter and smiling. I stared at him and said, "Sorry, I do not know you."

He replied with a smile, "Not yet."

Then, like a teenage girl, I said, "You are the 'Hotel California' guy."

He said, "What?"

"You were blasting it in your car the other day," I replied.

He smiled and started to unleash his massive knowledge of the Eagles onto me. I was captured in his stare, yes, and in his knowledge. This guy knew music. My *Rolling Stone* magazine was now talking to me, I thought. He stated he had to make some deliveries in town for his job and wanted my number. I gave him my number, and then he said, "Can I drive you home?"

"Next time," was my reply. My mind was in a spiral. I said "next time" to this stranger, a potential stalker, and thought, *What would the nuns think now?*

Within a few days, he called, and we were off on long drives, with loud music and many smiles. These drives were after he had finished his deliveries in town. I was eager for him to meet my best friend and sister, as I had such a wonderful time with him.

One day, we were out by his car, and my mom was standing in the front doorway. He said he wanted to meet her. I was very protective and started to brief him on my mom's struggles, but he was ahead of me, saying it would be fine. She smiled and shook his hand. The meeting was about two minutes long, and I informed her he was "just leaving." He asked me to return to his car, and sitting there in the seat across from me, he held out his arms in front of me. He was wearing a T-shirt. He asked, "Can you feel both of my arms at the same time?"

I said okay, and with both hands, I reached out and held his arms. My eyes popped out of my head. "Wow, why is one hot and one cold?" I asked.

"Did you know your mom is a witch?" he said.

"What?" I said. My mouth was hanging open, and in disbelief, I said, "No, you got that wrong. Alcoholic, yes; witch, no."

"Look it up," he said. I sat there staring at him. He said, "I am a warlock. I would know."

"A what?" I said. As my head was spinning, my heart sank, but that tingling was still there.

"Read up; you really need to know," he said.

"Since I was a little girl, I have had visions and dreams, and my parents never entertained this," I said. "They were against it, so if my mom was a witch, don't you think she would be more supportive?"

He looked at me and said, "You just do not understand." I got out of the car completely confused, with the lyrics of the Eagles song rolling around my mind.

"My head grew heavy, and my sight grew dim, / I had to stop for the night" was exactly how I was feeling.

Late that evening, after 10:00 p.m., I went to the *Encyclopedia Britannia* for answers to this new problem. My boyfriend and my mom were witches? I read everything I could. I had never seen or heard anything from my mother that resembled witchcraft. Like my father, she was Roman Catholic, and she was Irish. She was a proud graduate of Syracuse University and a member of the sorority Kappa Kappa Gamma. She started her career as a teacher, then worked as an editor for *Reader's Digest* magazine, where she met my father. She never mentioned anything like what I was reading in the encyclopedia. I trusted the information in the encyclopedia as this was our Google of the time. I told my sister and best friend, who were in disbelief and almost thought it laughable. I agreed to forget about it and vowed to never mention it again. The reality of my family having enough problems was already a good-enough answer for me. However, this boyfriend was right in my mind. I felt it, but with no proof other than his arm temperature, I was forced to forget it.

One day, my mom stood at the front door and mentioned the lyrics of a song about how "you can't hurry love." It stopped me in my tracks; I turned around. It was a 1960s Supremes hit song about waiting for love. I asked her what that was all about, and she told me I would figure it out. Within a brief period, there was a misunderstanding with the boyfriend about his whereabouts, and I decided to end it. It was a somewhat confusing time. Nevertheless, I knew that the oddity of my mom mentioning the lyrics of a sixties song and how haunted I was by "Hotel California" lyrics meant the relationship needed to end. That was 1984. A year later, in March of 1985, my mother died suddenly; I was sixteen years old. I never asked her about being a witch, but later in my life, certain events took place that hinted toward some evidence that the boyfriend was correct about her.

1985 felt surreal, as I started to live a life with only one parent. Music again became my friend. The band Simple Minds had an immensely popular song called "Don't You Forget about Me," featured in the movie *The Breakfast Club*. More than thirty years later, my sister and I often think about the trying time in our teenage lives when that song comes over the radio. As I wrote in my first book, *Seeing More than Clouds in Your Coffee*, sudden death is one of the most difficult experiences in life. Sudden death is an unanticipated death, which can leave loved ones in a state of shock. Even the death of a loved one who has spent months struggling in medical treatment sometimes feels like a surprise to those left behind. Even if we try to fully prepare ourselves for the death of a loved one, it can come as a terrible surprise. I have experienced the sudden death of a family member, stranger, friend, and patient. All these deaths were memorable, and no two were the same. Depending upon the circumstance, sudden death leaves loved ones with many unanswered questions. Feelings of frustration, doubt, and anger sometimes fill our hearts. All these sudden deaths are heartbreaking no matter the age, person, or circumstance. My mother was fifty-two years old; however, due to her struggle with alcohol, her body was much older. I cherish the good times and bad with her as they all served a purpose, and provided lessons and experience.

Learning lessons and forming experiences are usually the best memories of the teenage years. Some lessons are harder to learn than others, and you might tend to agree with that concept. However, thinking back on the growth during those teenage years, influences, good or bad, added to the experience and helped shape that road ahead. Although the nuns and I did not share the same total beliefs, I learned a tremendous amount from them.

One of the best lessons they taught me was to ask questions. Since many of them were retired teachers, they enjoyed explaining and giving examples to solve problems. I often thought of them many years later, especially while serving in Iraq. Critical decision-making, planning, and preparation were key throughout my tour in Iraq. Very often, we were expected to make decisions in an ever-changing environment, but I would reflect and think of them and the amount of faith they had amid the unknown. The army taught me about selecting the best course of action. As teenagers, we are usually only faced with one course of action; as we grow and expand, we realize that decisions need proper planning. Throughout high school, I focused on business courses until I realized, through my work at the convent, that I wanted to pursue nursing. The guidance counselor, who was a nun, told me I would not be selected for nursing school unless I added chemistry to my coursework. I did, and I realized I had added a second course of action for my future career choice by having been schooled in both science and business.

My senior year was terribly busy, as I was juggling both course tracks and taking track and field as an after-school activity. During this year, my best friend and I met some kids from our neighborhood, some of whom were still attending public school. These guys were quite different from us and were quite fun. Their ages ranged, but most were a year or two older or younger than us. The one common thread in each of them was their clear ability to look out for us like big brothers or new dads. They introduced us to music, people, and a way of life that we knew never to follow. Their big-brother-and-dad-like attitude enforced the concept that we should not follow their unruly behaviors, addictions, or confusion, but witness and avoid them. These guys filled a gap for me in understanding addiction, something I had always wanted to know from my mother, but she could never have that conversation. These guys were honest, caring, and forgiving of each other amid their own struggles. Their legal experiences and mishaps were never hidden from us, but discussed in a way to show how they narrowly escaped or were merely caught in the wrong place at the wrong time. These guys were in a drug rehabilitation program called Day Top, and my friend and I often volunteered to drop them off for their sessions.

Throughout high school, I always kept busy with coursework and work at the convent to stay out of any real trouble. I also was limited to getting involved in too much due to my mother's struggles and then my additional responsibilities after she suddenly passed away. My senior year was one of the most freeing times I experienced, especially with my new neighborhood music friends always finding time for me. They all looked like they stepped out of a movie set, wearing the heaviest of leather jackets, sporting long hair, and having their box-shaped radios with them as they were hanging around the local schoolyard smoking their cigarettes. Music from bands like Accept, Van Halen, Led Zeppelin, or even Alice Cooper flowed constantly out of their radio cassette players. What I learned from them was a different side of life. None of them had actual plans—no direction, no future—just that day, that time, and that space. I was not accustomed to this type of existence.

As much as I prodded my friends to discover their goals or plans, most of their outlooks on themselves were negative. I tried to offer guidance or support, or even help them envision something other than what did not interest them. I assumed what they had been telling me was correct: the bad influences, broken homes, and drugs changed their original paths in some way that made them feel this way. I gathered up enough courage to ask one of them, the guy I thought was my boyfriend, to my senior prom. I stood there staring into his eyes as a small smile glided across his face.

"Really," he said.

I said, "Really."

He was my senior prom date, and I could not be happier he said yes.

He cleaned up nicely—better than I expected; he almost resembled a hunky character from one of the 1970s hit shows. We shared a limo with another couple, and as we walked into the crowded venue, I noticed that many of the girls from my all-girls Catholic high school were astonished I was with him. Little did I know he was well known to them, especially to those who lived closer to New York City. How they knew him was not important as my mind started to speculate. I blocked those negative thoughts and returned to the room as the strobe lights and glitter surrounded me. This scene was reminiscent of the mixers we attended throughout the years, just with fancier clothing. I had so many smiling faces turn my way, and I felt just as good as I did when I demonstrated the tobacco in ninth grade.

What my prom date did for me that night was the same thing I had done for him throughout the school year while hanging out in the schoolyard and on Day Top rides. He listened, supported, and encouraged me. I knew that although we lived different lives, we could still be friends. To this day, I often think back on those innocent times and years. There was always an invisible difference between us. The difference was in our plans for the future or ideas of what we wanted. In many of these guys' favorite songs, the concept of death and taking chances was always somehow lingering in the background and often woven in their lives, like in the lyrics of an often-played Motorhead song "The Ace of Spades:" "But that's the way I like it, baby / I don't wanna live forever."

Looking back at the reality they showed me, I realized it reflected the same concept of life and death paired in their song choices. Just like in the song, the ace of spades in a regular playing deck of cards is seen as death.

About fifteen years ago, I called a Yonkers cab company. As I sat in the backseat, I looked up. Familiar eyes stared at me in the rearview mirror, and I heard the driver say, "Cath, is that you?" It was Frankie McGuire, one of the guys from this crowd of leather-jacketed friends.

"Frankie, oh wow, how are you?" I asked.

"Good, I am driving you around," he said, laughing. He rattled off some names from the past as he started to drive down the street reminiscing.

As I was getting out at my destination, I said, "It's good to see you."

"It's good we are still alive," he said, smiling.

From time to time when I needed a cab, Frankie would take my pickup and we would catch up. Just a few years ago, I heard Frankie died at home suddenly. I was stunned, along with many others. I was happy about our ride conversations and the chance to reconnect with someone I thought I would never see again. Frankie was always looking out for me as a teen and years later during those cab rides. He would offer his brotherly advice, especially about dating, tell me funny jokes, and always tell me to smile. Death comes for all of us, sometimes quicker and more unexpected than planned; there is no escape from it. Some of these guys have since died, like Frankie, as I understand, while others have miraculously found themselves, like me, thankfully still alive.

Chapter 3

Many of you might remember the 1980s well. It was a time of a lot of activity and change and left me with many memories. According to history, the time between 1979 and 1991 is known as the late stage of the Cold War. There was increased hostility between the West and the Soviet Union. The 1980s were notably tough. In 1981, President Reagan was shot by a lone shooter, a crazed fan. Dad was a huge fan of the president, often explaining to us what was happening politically and how things were being handled. He enjoyed politics, but he also gave his own opinion about events. Tensions overseas were running high, and my senior trip to Germany was canceled in 1986 due to bombing activity. This left us the consolation prize of a ski trip. My dad was equally anxious for our safety and happy since he had been an avid skier and thought it was the perfect selection. Dad was a huge fan of the nuns, so their decisions always seemed right to him.

Many are surprised to hear I have served in the military. People ask me many questions about how, when, and where I joined. Thinking back, I remember meeting members of the military at a career fair I attended while in high school. These guys were great recruiters and spoke highly of serving. Although I knew it was a fantastic opportunity, I kept that idea tucked in the back of my mind. At that time, I knew I could not just pick up and leave after graduation with the new adjustment in our family after my mom passed away.

By 1990, I was a registered nurse in Yonkers and wanted to further my nursing education with a bachelor's degree. Many of the possibilities for financial assistance were not available to me, so I set off to discover what the military could offer. Some of my friends had served in the Gulf War and returned with details of their experiences, all of which were quite different depending on their position and location. I initially thought I would join the United States Navy after speaking to my father, who served with them from 1946 to 1948. The navy informed me they would make me a medical specialist and not a nurse. The navy's policy was that anyone who wanted to join the Nurse Corps had to already hold a bachelor's degree. I was already a registered nurse in the state of New York, but I only held an associate degree in nursing.

I looked puzzled at hearing this information but standing in the doorway across the hallway was an army sergeant with the thickest of southern accents. As he was leaning against the frame of the door, the army sergeant explained to me with a smile that the Army Reserve would take me as a nurse and pay me to get a bachelor's degree. My eyes lit up, and with a smile, I marched across the hallway to see what he was promising. I made it clear to him that I wanted to join the navy since my father served in the navy. He informed me that was a long time ago, which was true. I knew I needed a bachelor's degree to be a charge nurse at my civilian hospital. He smiled and said, "Go home and tell Dad what I said."

I came home and brought up the topic to Dad. He seemed surprised that I had gone down to the recruiting station in south Yonkers alone, but he sat in silence and listened. As I rolled out the details of what the navy and army staff had told me, he seemed to lean forward in his chair. I asked him his opinion. He said, "Well, sounds like you are making the right choice with the Army Reserve." I looked shocked as if I were expecting a different answer and reaction from him. He knew this was the best course of action. The pros outweighed the cons in this situation, and Dad was a smart man.

You must understand that I was signing on for eight years of work; in the army's eyes, however, I was signing on for a fourteen-year commitment. They were correct. It is "army math," I was told, and would ease the uncertainty of a long commitment. My contract stated eight years plus six years for education, which was two years for every one year of college. The army math totals to a fourteen-year commitment. The fourteen years seemed steep, but I was young and only twenty-two years old. I signed on the dotted line, raised my hand, and took the oath. At that time, I had no idea what my military career could teach and provide me.

Before I knew it, I started learning and fulfilling all the commitments to match the promises the Army Reserve gave me. The army encouraged pursuing higher degrees as they ensured a good chance of being promoted. I spent most of the 1990s with my nose to the grindstone of work and study, which, looking back, paid off. One of the best lessons I have learned in life is to listen to advice, especially when you think it sounds impossible or even like a challenge. It was just these challenges that pushed me through the many civilian and military courses. As I worked hard throughout the 1990s, the army trained me in various positions in health care, mostly in critical care and leadership. Most of the years after graduating from nursing school were focused on working in the Army Reserve and furthering my education.

Toward the end of the 1990s, I began to instruct in the military, which I loved instantly. The army certifies you to instruct on anything. There is a certain way the army teaches instruction and public speaking, and I believe they do it very well. The army's course on becoming an instructor is precise and is based on communication, which is key in instructing anything. I was pleased to launch into teaching, something I had done minimally at that point in my life.

My father was my first instructor in life. He had been a certified National Rifle Association (NRA) firearms instructor, and he took that job very seriously when teaching me to shoot at age nine. Dad was a subject matter expert with rifles. He taught me everything about the rifle, from its manufacture to safety to the precision of firing it. My first rifle was a .22-caliber target rifle, which I mastered quickly. Within a brief period, he introduced me to a .270 rifle. With his guidance and patience, I mastered that one. For those of you reading who do not know about shooting, there is a significant difference in firepower, especially for a nine-year-old. Just to give you an idea about the difference between the rifles, the .22 long rifle is effective in shooting up to one hundred fifty yards while the .270 is effective up to five hundred yards. Dad stated that the most important thing in teaching is to know your subject always. He was right; the more I taught for the army, the more I realized I needed to become the subject matter expert (SME) to be considered one of the best.

One of the best ways to be an instructor is to know your audience. I learned this after several years of instructing. During my time as a lieutenant colonel, the military advanced me to the position of senior trainer. Several times throughout my career, I have had to help coach other instructors and show them how to prepare for teaching different blocks of instruction. I made it a habit to remind them to change their methods of teaching to match their audiences. The audience, or in our case our soldier students, all learn differently and in a variety of ways.

One method of teaching was to find out what they did in their civilian careers, to better understand how they could learn. I realize how many of the soldiers had civilian jobs that were exceedingly difficult. Many of our staff had stellar careers in tough jobs that included law enforcement, firefighting, health care, and construction. While instructing, we learned that very few students had ever thought of themselves as instructors. After speaking with them, they realized they were instructing every day, just in different ways on their civilian jobs.

As senior instructors, we often reminded students to stay flexible in any environment. I often used my deployment to Iraq as an example of being flexible and creative. In 2004, my division was asked to go to Iraq as instructors, advisers, and leaders. We did, and all but five of us returned. Training occurred inside or outside of buildings and in and among imminent fire and danger. We instructed interpreters by our sides to ensure accuracy and understanding. One crucial point is to always prepare for the unexpected and use everything to your advantage, always making changes to suit the allowable time to instruct. Some of us used different training experiences to highlight instructing in a different terrain or country. I often reflected on my experience in 2012 when my unit was sent to train the Jordanian army and all the instruction was based outside during winter.

These overseas experiences were enlightening to us as trainers. Often during these experiences, we shared stories of our careers, families, or even other deployments. A few times, we would discuss how we were notified that we were going to a combat zone. In my case, I shared when I was informed that I was going to Iraq. Many of my fellow officers found my story remarkably funny: I told them a psychic told me first. In March of 2004, I attended a local psychic fair run by my friend Vince. He set up on alternating Sundays at local hotels in New York and New Jersey so the public to have readings throughout the month.

One Sunday, I sat with my friend Louise, who was one of his long-standing psychics. She said that in about six months or so, I would be going on a trip far away. I can still hear her say in her thick New York accent, “Like far, Cath—like overseas.”

I laughed and said, “I am not going anywhere like that.” I reminded her that many in New York were still shaken from the aftermath of 9/11.

Leaning over the table, which was covered in a colorful shawl, she said in an exceptionally whispery voice, “What about the army?”

I said, “No, we are a training division.” I reassured her that would never happen. At the time, it was not common for training divisions to be sent in that manner. Historically, training divisions trained stateside those who were scheduled to go down range. The rest of her reading was spot on; she touched on the details about the New York City cop I had started dating and about my work that all seemed correct with her usual accuracy.

We were friends even outside of these Sundays, so I planned to haunt her in six months or so with the item that never came true. As a child, I had many perfectly accurate visions, mostly about everyone else but me. In my life, seeing my future or my upcoming events does not easily occur, and as Louise would remind me, that was a “good thing.”

One day, I was so frustrated with her, I said, “Don’t you think we as psychics should know what will happen to our futures?”

Louise, an immensely proud Italian who was always pleasant and cheerful, rolled her eyes in my direction and said, "Listen, Cath, you wouldn't leave your bed in the morning."

Yet again, Louise spoke the truth. In July, we were told that our unit would be headed to Iraq by October. We would be the first training division to serve as reservists in Iraq as part of the rebuilding plan after the invasion in 2003. Apparently, our division was making history doing this under General Petraeus. I phoned Louise; I was not halfway through my story when she reminded me that she was always right in her predictions. Louise did not stop there. She immediately connected her phone to a three-way call to invite another psychic named John to investigate my situation further. I had never met John, but he made a few statements about the army officers I knew and worked with, which were all true. He rambled out some quick sentences that I jotted down, and none of it made sense. She was confident after the call ended that, eventually, I was going to be okay.

I have not always been open about my psychic abilities; it was a concept I struggled with for years. I struggled with how others would see me, judge me, and accept me. As you have already read, I was raised in a Roman Catholic home, which was clearly against having this ability. I often thought the military could be problematic as well. I understood that the military was involved in investigating psychic phenomena between the 1950s and 1990s, but the details of this work were unknown to me. What was more important to me was how I would be perceived as a senior leader with a known psychic ability. I was just unsure.

Louise and John were correct with their statement about me returning home. His confusing sentences that I jotted down came true as well, but over time while I was in Iraq. My father experienced a sudden heart complication, which forced me to return home for my two weeks' leave, but as John mentioned, he would be okay. He also mentioned some construction issues regarding my home. While I was away, my sister inspected my apartment, collected my mail, and ensured my car battery did not die. On one of her trips through my apartment, she found that the bathroom ceiling plaster had come down, requiring her to arrange a construction repair. John had also mentioned that the cop I was dating was not long-term, and that too proved to be true.

While in Iraq, several events occurred that were completely psychic in nature. These events I found hard to explain to others and difficult to personally experience. One of the biggest events occurred after I had been in the country less than a week. I warned an officer who was headed out one morning on a convoy. I approached him by rank and name and told him to "be safe." He did not understand me reaching out until several hours later when his convoy was hit. In these early days of the war, the vehicles in our convoys were not armored, and we were riding around in vehicles like Nissan Pathfinders. In this officer's convoy, two of the four occupants were injured, but all thankfully survived. This officer was fine, and two injured officers received Purple Heart awards. I met up with all of them the following day.

When we spoke, he questioned how I sensed the danger around him. I explained I have a gift but wanted to reassure him he would be fine, and they all immediately thanked me. Several years later, I ran into this officer at a training event. I was so proud to see he was promoted and still serving. He was excited to see me and tell me about his career, family, and life after Iraq. He was completely at peace with the details of the event and excited about his life and future.

After I returned from Iraq, one of my battle buddies from Iraq asked me to share my psychic ability with the public. I was torn emotionally over making this commitment since I was fearful of the perception. However, internally, I knew that sharing my gift would bring me more into the public eye, exposing this part of my belief system and practice to the outside world. I also knew that working with my abilities publicly would pull me out of my loneliness. One would think I would be pleased by that, but at times, my loneliness was a comfort and a friend as I have always struggled with change. I decided the only way forward was to be myself; and being myself was being the registered nurse, the army officer, and the psychic medium. All these roles involved caring, and I needed to be true to myself to also care for myself.

I made it a point to inform the army leaders, my commanders, and at times even the commanding generals, of my psychic work. The main point of informing them was because I was being asked to do radio shows, and some of the projects had some media involvement. The media involvement was especially based on the paranormal field. Overall, they all took it in stride, seemed unrattled, and more importantly, were more impressed with my military skills. Their understanding of my roles in life instantly gave me the confidence to move forward with my plans.

Occasionally, a skeptic would question my psychic work or my choice of doing this work and remind me of my military rank. Surprisingly, some would even demand a response from me. My response was always, "It's amazing to me that you seem to have a problem with it since my unit commander doesn't." I would smile and then wait for a further response, but that usually would quiet them down. In life, we all face fear. Sometimes we learn the lesson that the issue we most fear tends to be nothing worth fearing.

Chapter 4

You never know sometimes how long friendships will last. My oldest friendship is with my friend Cookie. We met in the fourth grade in our Catholic grammar school. Cookie and I shared many experiences throughout our lifetimes. Even at an early age, Cookie shared some of my same beliefs and interests. We consulted each other on our aquariums, cats, and even our choices. As preteens, part of the best decision-making for us involved using a pendulum, which to our amazement somehow gave us the correct choices. In my eyes, Cookie was extremely intuitive and was often trying to talk me out of a decision or choice as she was much "wiser." I can still hear her say, "I do not know if you really want to do that." More times than I would like to admit, she was right, but remembering some of my crazy ideas and antics is fun.

One of the best gifts Cookie shared with me was her mom. Cookie's mother, Maga, whom I have mentioned in my first book *Seeing More than Clouds in Your Coffee*, was like a second mother to me. She has come to me often since she passed, always with clear messages. I pass those messages and images on to Cookie, as they often have nothing to do with me but very much to do with Cookie or her family. Maga believed in the afterlife and found the work of mediums fascinating. Maga enjoyed following John Edward in the television show *Crossing Over*. She enjoyed him so much since he was one of the few who incorporated the Roman Catholic religion into his practice and often spoke of praying the rosary. Maga was a devoted Catholic and prayed the rosary.

My mother and Maga were vastly different although they shared the same astrological sign of the Taurus. Maga was so open; she would often tell us stories and share her common interests with us, which mostly involved watching *General Hospital*, shopping, and her family. Maga opened her heart to everyone she met. She helped her family and those in her church the most. There was not a time I remember her ever saying no to anyone. She would find time, move her schedule around, and always be her amazing creative self. My mother was quite the opposite. As much as my mom was social and helpful, there was a lingering quietness to her that often captured my attention. Perhaps the quietness was clouded by her alcohol addiction or stressors she held deep inside, but there were some great lessons that she taught me. I wish I had learned more about her living life, but I am grateful for some great gifts she left me. The following story reflects upon one of those gifts.

Sometimes people ask me for my assistance in a matter when they are truly struggling with an issue or concern. I once was involved with a family where the mother and her sister were terribly upset with a daughter who was pregnant. This was an unplanned teen pregnancy and seemed to create drama for the family. The family were upset by it and were finding it hard to have any deep discussion. I was invited to meet them and create a discussion to see how I could help.

I gathered that somehow the mother and her sister seemed to be involved in discussing name choices for the baby. The young mom was discussing naming the baby after the absent father, and this seemed to upset the mother and her sister immensely. I could see the panic rising in the mother's eyes, so I offered to tell the family a personal story. I gently asked the young mother if she had thought of any songs for the baby. This statement quieted the chatter in the room.

I expressed that my mother often mentioned how she selected two famous songs that seemed to resonate with her for my sister and me when we were little. My mom selected "Raindrops Keep Fallin' on My Head," written by Burt Bacharach and Hal David and featured in the 1969 film *Butch Cassidy and the Sundance Kid,* for my sister. She selected the 1970 song "Close to You" by the Carpenters for me. Both songs were big hits at the time, and it is apparent she did not give these to us as infants but as toddlers. My mother always told us that she found it a thrill to assign songs to us when we were little so that in later years, we would know she chose those songs personally for us. It was the perfect lifetime gift she gave us. The songs were iconic to the time and perfectly chosen; both reflected being upbeat and wrapped up in hope and promise for the future.

The young mom did not recognize the songs, but the mother and her sister did. With a smile, they asked the young mom, "Well, what song would you like to choose?"

The young mom smiled and said, "Wow, there are just so many."

When I walked out into the hallway with the mother, she said to me, "How did you do that?"

I said a major part of friendship is sharing, not just caring. Years later, I still retell that story whenever there is a family who is struggling. During stress, it is often difficult to see both sides of any situation, especially when the stress is occurring within the same household, which could lead to even more difficulties. The gift that my mother gave me was a song, but the impact of that gift has been a gift to so many others. My mother lived a short life, but it was rich in detail and creativity. Her one act of song creativity has rippled like a wave through many families, and for that I am delighted.

Throughout the years of doing mediumship readings, I have found that many families struggle with communication. In my experience, the most difficult readings are those I read when they are grieving the loss of a child. In my opinion, there is no grief more heartbreaking than the loss of a child, no matter the age of that child. Communication within the family, especially before, during, and after the loss of a child, becomes the focal point for families, especially the parents. Some families ponder if their child understood their love, reflect on their discipline, or wonder about choices that were made throughout an illness or addiction. The mediumship readings provide evidence of spirit as well as messages from their loved ones. Offering comfort, support, love, and resources is imperative to these families throughout their incredible grief.

My first personal experience with a child's death occurred when I was about nine or ten years old. I was a patient in the local hospital, and I had my appendix removed. Back in those days, they would keep children in the hospital for about a week for this type of surgical procedure. I remember my hospital stay vividly. The pediatric ward had rooms lined up on both sides of the hallway with glass windows in between. My father had been a hospital corpsman in the United States Navy in the late1940s, so he sat by my bedside and explained the procedure to me. He decided he would come daily and read to me *Captains Courageous*, an 1897 novel by Rudyard Kipling that he loved. I remember meeting two girl patients slightly older than me in the dayroom. The dayroom was a large children's room with toys, arts, and crafts that overlooked the Hudson River.

When my dad left that early evening before the surgery, the girls came into my room. They immediately showed me how to lower the side rails on my bed and walked me down to find the bathroom in the hallway. They even took me into a room that had a telephone and told me I could dial my parents on it. On our way back to my room, I asked them why they were showing me all this stuff.

"Because the nurses here will not help you," one said. I was shocked, and I felt awful. I did not want to believe it.

I got in my bed, and one lifted the rail and said, "If you do not believe us, that is fine, but a boy died in your very own bed before you came here."

The other girl chimed in by saying, "They could not help him even though they tried." The two girls in their hospital gowns left.

I lay there in my bed, horrified, but they were right, and I knew it. Even on the tour of our hospital pediatric ward, no nurse stopped us, and none of the nurses were even looking for us.

I pictured a boy in my mind. Oddly enough, I felt like I could see what he looked like. I felt like he was feeling helpless just like I did now. I wondered why my dad did not know about this mistreatment by the nurses. I pulled at the sheets and saw that the plastic mattress cover was of a maroon-red color and that instantly reminded me of the color of blood. This vision, paired with the sad story of the boy, filled my mind with horrid thoughts. That experience motivated me to get well fast and get home as soon as possible. I did not tell my dad any of this since I did not want to worry him. I just told him to take me home every night he came to visit and read to me.

"Soon enough," he would say and get into the chapter where we had left off. I did go home with my surgical dressing in place, a new love of life, and an appreciation for health and home. Those little girls were telling the truth, and I knew it. I do not believe they were out to scare me but, in their way, to enlighten me about life. Not surprisingly, later in my days of nurse's training in the same hospital, I often reflected on that experience, and always raced to answer call bells and carefully listen to the patients. I learned quickly that patients provide many clues to their care and condition, especially post-op or during chemotherapy.

During my early teens, my father and his work friend and I would go shooting at an outdoor range. During these fantastic range days, the two of them would discuss work; they would lean over and give me tips for sighting in my rifle and helping me enhance my breathing. These range days always ended with a trip to the diner and a warm cup of coffee. They would ramble on and laugh, telling stories. His friend was such a great guy and was the father of three boys. I remember he was always smiling. I often wanted to interrupt them and ask about his kids, but he and Dad were always in such deep conversations it never felt important enough. I wondered if his boys ever went shooting with him and often wondered why he never brought them along. I gathered from bits and pieces that they were quite the athletes and always doing some sports thing. I knew why this man spent time together with us since Dad was an incredible shooter. Anyone who ever spent time with my dad on the range knew the time, precision, and patience that he had. I was never that still and easily learned to stop talking or "thinking out loud" as Dad would joke. This man was also in Dad's league of shooting regarding accuracy and skill. He often consulted him and reflected on the missed shots, listening for Dad's words of wisdom.

One night, my dad came home from work and looked awful. I asked him what happened, but he could hardly speak. He sat down, and with his hands on his forehead, he repeated the story he had heard at work. The sixteen-year-old son of our range friend, his coworker, had died. I sat down and tried to listen, but I kept seeing our range friend across the diner table with his hot cup of coffee in hand and a brilliant smile.

"What happened?" I asked.

Dad retold a story that ended with a bunch of kids in a car after a sporting event. They were all killed instantly. Dad and I attended the wake. It was located "up the line," as Dad called north of where we lived. We got to the funeral home, and I had never seen such a massive crowd. The line we stood in went down the street and around the building. We waited and listened to the sniffling, crying, and small chatter of those in the line with us. Dad and I were silent. Although I did not know his son, I felt incredibly sad, seeing the boy's friends and families in attendance.

Once inside the parlor, we met up with our range friend who was unrecognizable. The face I was accustomed to was gone, and I felt the heavy emotion when I saw my dad hug him instead of his usual handshake greeting. On the long drive home, Dad spoke of the importance of driving and reflected on his early days of race car driving. He always stressed the importance of managing a vehicle, anticipating other vehicles, and controlling yourself while driving. He stressed how easily you can become distracted by yourself or others. He mentioned a few graphic events that occurred throughout his racing career, at events, where some of his friends—experienced racers—were instantly killed. He mentioned he would not be surprised if our range friend never returned to the range. Dad was right; we never did have another range day with him. We continued to go, but it was much different. He was sadly missed, but we understood completely.

Children—we all get that title at one time in our lives. However, not everyone chooses to have children. But the definition of *children* is very broad, in my own opinion. During a recent mediumship reading, I was reading for a gentleman, who was validating his family members as I brought them through. Some of the messages were comical, showing the personality of one of his relatives. Toward the end of the reading, I paused and said, "I have your son. He is giving me such a warm sensation, and I am surrounded by love. He tells me about the adventures you had and the walks you would take."

The man looked confused and started to say, "I am sorry, I don't think you have that right."

I said, "I do. He was your dog."

The man stared and shook his head. He continued with, "No, I haven't had a dog. Well, since…" He paused.

I said, "That's right; you were about nine or ten years old."

At that point, tears began to stream down his face, and he said, "That's right, that's my Sonny." He explained that his dad would call him Sonny. When the man got the dog, he called the dog Sonny because he thought that was what all dads did. He was the dad to this dog even though he was still the child in the family. The man continued to tell me how long he had the dog, how that dog shared all his secrets and knew all his fibs. The man admitted the incredible grief he had when the dog passed. It was so deep, he suppressed it and forced himself not to deal with it. As an older teen, he got involved with life and pushed it down deep. The reading, he said, helped him remember his Sonny and be grateful for his friendship and camaraderie.

Frankie McGuire (RIP)
photo taken as a teen
in Yonkers, NY

Frankie McGuire (RIP) photo taken in 2014 Chauffeur/ Dispatch at Break to the Border Car & Limo Service Yonkers, NY

Shooting with Dad at Blue Mountain Sportsman Center Cortland Manor, NY 1995

Shooting pistols (NRA) at Women's Wilderness Escape at the Whittington Center, Raton New Mexico 2016

Shooting rifles (NRA) at Women's Wilderness Escape at the Whittington Center Raton, New Mexico 2016

Long range shooting school (300-1000 yards) with Outdoor Solutions in Coalville, Utah June 2022

Joining the US Army Reserve 1991 COL Samuel C. Berte`(RIP)
from White Plains, NY commissioned me

1LT Nadal in Officer Advanced
School San Antonio, Texas

Major Nadal in Baghdad, Iraq 2005

LTC Nadal teaching Military Decision Making Process (MDMP) in Ft. Dix, NJ 2014

COL Nadal in Washington DC, just after reading the names at the Vietnam Wall 2017

COL Nadal retires
June 2021

Home on leave from Iraq, having lunch in Brooklyn, NY 2005 with My Uncle Henry (RIP) Cousin Anthony (RIP) and Dad (RIP)

Dad in the U.S. Navy

Dad

Dad and me on the Brooklyn Bridge

Maga Cookie's Mom (Mary Grubiak) (RIP)

My Mom Emily McPartland Nadal (RIP)

My good friend and fellow psychic Louise Johnson (RIP)

Feb 16th

To Cathy dear –

Always remember we love you so dearly.

I'm sure your retreat will be a most interesting experience. Life is an adventure and you will find it most rewarding.

Our prayers are with you constantly.

All our love –

Mommy + Daddy

P.S. (Remember the song "On the day you were born"

Chapter 5

A couple of years after returning from Iraq, I was doing a bit of my own soul-searching. I attended two sessions over a two-year period with the shaman Clay Lomakayu Miller in Cottonwood, Arizona. A good friend recommended Clay as a spiritual healer, as he uses a unique form of healing called "soul dreaming." Clay has worked with many people, including celebrities, on many different issues. I was curious. The process of soul dreaming is to free yourself from your past in order to be able to share your gift with the world. Clay is a delightful man who is incredibly gifted and grounded.

When I first met Clay, he informed me I would be at his home for two-hour sessions for three days. On the final day, we would hike into the mountains for the final session. He creates a circle on the rug with his Akita dogs surrounding him, as they too are part of the process of centering and providing love. The sessions with Clay were recorded on a CD. He combines the session with a hot stone, channeling, and playing a whimsical flute. Clay speaks about "blocks" and finds out if you are aware or unaware of your blocks. Blocks stop you from being your true self. I was not sure I had a block, but within minutes of hearing Clay channel me, which was something I had never experienced before, I understood. At that time in my life, I felt stuck. I often told friends, "I can't," either giving them excuses of being busy with the army, caring for Dad, or just being tired. I said, "I can't" to everything, and that was my block.

Between the sessions spread out over a three-day period, I realized the progress I had made. By the completion of final day, I was no longer saying, "I can't," and Clay was able to get to the significant part of why I was still feeling blocked. During the second journey with Clay, my block was judgment. I grew up with judgment; it surrounded me as a child with an alcoholic mom and a workaholic dad. I had become an overachiever in life. I raced through so many items on my wish list for both my civilian and military careers that I had not carved out a true personal life. I struggled with my psychic gift and was fearful of judgment for being who I truly was.

Looking back, now over a decade or so later, I know Clay fixed that. He would suggest that I fixed it. He looked into my eyes, told me why I was on the earth, and reminded me why I needed to be here. In his own way, he informed me about the hardest judge in my life: me. I needed to stop. He was correct. I remember as he was talking to me on top of the mountain on the last day about this. One of the dogs walked over and lay at my feet. We were standing and looking down at his dog. He informed me that his dogs were his helpers in this work, and his dog was sending me the signal to just surrender myself and to let go of the judgment. Clay teaches you about the circle and how that circle is about healing, forgiveness, and the truth. I reflected on my two sessions over the two-year period and how completely different they were. I was astounded at how the healing was in the true sense of the word and the work done throughout the sessions. I needed to do the three Fs: to forgive, forget, and forge on to the future.

I began to work at psychic fairs and attend psychic development classes and sessions. After studying with Suzane Northrop and James Van Praagh, I wanted to know how I could be evaluated by British standards. I attended the Arthur Findlay College in Stansted, England, to learn more about the advancement in spiritualism and psychic sciences. I studied with medium-tutor Simone Key twice, several years apart. Attendance at the college and the evaluation by British standards felt important to me as I understood the history of the school and their religion of spiritualism.

After attending, I applied to work in Salem, Massachusetts for the Halloween season. Salem, Massachusetts, is known as the Halloween capital of the world. People flock to Salem throughout the year to learn about the history, see the shops, and meet the witches. However, if you have never been to Salem during Halloween, you must make the trip; it is monumental. I was honored to be selected to work as a psychic medium in Salem for two different store owners from 2011 to 2018.

During the first year working there, I met with another psychic medium who was also a witch. During a quick conversation, she confirmed what the "Hotel California" boyfriend had told me years before. I stood staring at her when she mentioned that my gift came from my mother, who was unable to use it in her lifetime, and that it was important that I continue to use my gift. I mentioned to her that, when I was in in high school, a guy told me the exact same thing she did. I explained he felt that I "needed to know." She agreed. They both knew that my mother was unable to address this with me or even with herself. I welcomed this information as I had done extensive research on both sides of my family, and I have not found anyone other than me with this gift.

I began to study with Reverend Lori Bruno, a high priestess and elder of the Sicilian Strega line of the Craft of the Wise and founder of Our Lord and Lady of the Trinacrian Rose. Lori is a descendant of Giordano Bruno, who was born in 1548 in Nola, Italy, and was burned to death on February 17, 1600, at Campo de' Fiori in Rome. Lori's best friend was the well-known Leo Louis Martello, an American Wiccan priest and gay-rights activist. Lori thought of him as a brother, and has missed him dearly since he sadly passed on June 29, 2000. Leo is known for his several books, which have been instrumental for those studying witchcraft. Some of his books are *Witchcraft: The Old Religion*, *The Weird Ways of Witchcraft*, and *It's in the Cards*. Lori is incredibly gifted and has been named as a character in several of Patricia Cornwell's books of crime fiction. From the first time I met Lori in 2011, she was like a mother to me, and she still is. Many of us affectionately called her "Mama." We share telepathy with each other when she calls me, and I call her. It is uncanny, and she often says, "I knew you were calling me."

I remember telling her about the suggestion of my mother reflecting on the conversations with the psychic medium witch in Salem and the "Hotel California" boyfriend. Lori smiled and, with her strong New York accent, belted out with a smile, "Of course she was." I have learned so much from Lori Bruno, especially about understanding our responsibilities and dedication to our work as psychic mediums. Lori has explained her work as a WITCH, using an acronym she coined in her late teens. She created the acronym to give a definition of who we are and represent: Wisdom, Integrity, Truth, Courage, and Honor. I joined Our Lord and Lady of the Trinacrian Rose Church in 2019 and became a reverend.

Lori was one of the pivotal people who helped me understand my gift and the concept of judgment. In 2012, I applied to be certified as a medium with the Forever Family Foundation (FFF), a not-for-profit all-volunteer organization based in New York. It was founded by Bob Ginsberg and his late wife Phran Ginsberg; their purpose is to educate the public that we are more than our physical bodies. The entire medium certification process is a detailed evaluation of the evidence communicated by mediums. I completed an extensive application and was interviewed on the telephone. Several months later, I was asked to give a series of readings by phone and Skype. At the time, Skype was comparable to the Zoom of today. The process is conducted under controlled conditions, and the standards for certification are high. I was incredibly open with them from the start. I told them about my work in Salem and that I am a Wiccan. FFF's focus is on the proficiency of the medium, so this was not an issue. After the half day of readings, I was informed I would be notified by mail if I were accepted. About two weeks later, I received the letter of acceptance in the mail. The first person I phoned was my father. He had heard me speak about them in numerous conversations and was extremely impressed that I was selected.

Psychic mediums in FFF volunteer throughout the year to help the organization either by donating a reading for a raffle, attending a radio show, or working at one of the grief retreats. It is an honor to be affiliated with such a uniquely talented group of individuals all working toward the common goal of educating and informing people, and understanding the afterlife. Our work as mediums is based on providing support and guidance through messages of evidence of spirit to loved ones during the grief process.

During the time when I first joined the Forever Family Foundation, I met Doug Day. Doug was a well-known sound engineer and had worked in the music business since the late 1980s. He was known for his work with Solid State Logic (SSL). Meeting Doug was an amazing experience. We had many common friends and, oddly enough, many of the same interests, one of which was cars. Within the first week of meeting Doug, we walked down to the village and sat in a café shop for hours and spoke. I handed him a greeting card with the exact lines of a song that he loved. His eyes became bright and almost misty. He knew he found someone who listened to him. That started our two-year relationship that involved so many life lessons for both of us.

Doug was in the middle of clearing out the home he grew up in on Long Island as his mother was being cared for in a nearby nursing facility. Going through years of stuff was hard for Doug, and I understood why. He read my book *Seeing More than Clouds in Your Coffee* but often informed me that he did not have much belief in the afterlife. He even went on to say he did not have much belief in anything. I always looked disappointed, and he would smile and quickly say, “But it is okay that you do.”

We worked out our life balance between our two apartments and his motorcycle garage in Poughkeepsie. Many of the best memories we shared were with his dog Bowie. Bowie was his dog, a husky he got when he was just a pup. Doug named Bowie after David Bowie since they both had one blue eye and one brown eye. Doug and Bowie were a team, a paired set, and devoted friends. All the studios that Doug worked in knew Bowie and loved having him there alongside Doug. Once, in his apartment, Doug was sweeping up Bowie’s fur and said, “You know, I was thinking—you knit, right?”

I looked up and said, “You know I do.”

He smiled and said, “We can send Bowie’s fur out, and they can make yarn of it, and you can make me a Bowie sweater.” I thought he was joking, but a few days later, he had found a place online offering those exact services. This is just one example of Doug’s inventive mind and his love for Bowie.

Doug took me to the most incredible places, especially bars throughout New York City. He always had a wonderful story of events and times he had when he had been there in the past. On one special night, we were leaving a steakhouse around Eighteenth Street and started to walk through the Gramercy Park neighborhood. Walking down the street, Doug, being his supercool self, gently nodded his head and said to a tall man walking his two small dogs, "Hey, man."

After we passed, Doug said that was Ric Ocasek from The Cars. I spun around and waved and yelled, "Hey, hi!" Ric smiled, threw up a wave, and entered the apartment building. Doug was laughing, and we sang "Just What I Needed" by The Cars all the way home to his apartment on East Twenty-Second Street. To this day, when I hear that song come over the radio, I whisper and laugh and say, "Hey, hi."

Doug was a complete sport when I dragged him to see Rick Springfield at a book signing at the Barnes & Noble in Union Square. Once we got close to Rick and he was about to sign my book, Rick pointed to Doug and said, "Hey, you look like me, man."

Doug smiled and said, "That's what she says." They both laughed.

One morning, I woke up to a text message from my friend Cliff's son stating Cliff was in the hospital with a sudden medical condition. I immediately told Doug since Cliff was the twin brother of Glenn McLarnon and they had been featured in my first book, *Seeing More than Clouds in Your Coffee*. Glenn died suddenly in 2009, and Doug and I had discussed the McLarnon twins a lot since they had worked in Sam Ash in the early 1990s. Doug believed they shared some common friends. Doug immediately said we would visit Cliff that night after work. I was shocked but happy.

Once we got to the medical center, we spoke to Cliff at his bedside. Doug and Cliff spoke about their common friends from Sam Ash. Cliff mentioned Glenn's name a lot, told funny stories, and talked about jobs they had been assigned in the industry. Walking down the hallway to the elevator, I joked with Doug that I felt like Doug knew him for years. Once in the elevator, Doug pressed the button for the lobby; but a medical staff member stepped in, causing the doors to hesitate. Once in, she pressed her floor number and then peered out of the doors and screamed to a guy in scrubs passing by the closing doors, "Hey, Glenn!"

Doug looked down at me with the biggest eyes. I said, "Did you hear that?"

He immediately said yes. It looked like Doug was in shock. Walking out of the hospital and into the parking lot, I explained that is how it happens. I informed Doug about signs from the afterlife and how our loved ones stay connected. I explained how many signs Cliff has gotten and even the amazing dreams he has had when Glenn has visited him. Doug took it all in but still seemed leery.

One morning, we were in his apartment on Twenty-Second Street, and Doug sat up in bed and said, "Do you hear that? There it goes again." I looked at him, confused. "It is an owl," he said, smiling. "Here in New York City." He explained he heard an owl at his motorcycle shop in Poughkeepsie all the time, but hearing one in New York City was wild to him.

I told him about animal totems and the amazing author Ted Andrews. I told him the symbolism of the owl. According to Ted, the owl is a spirit animal that guides you to see beyond the veil of deception and illusion and often helps you to see what is being kept hidden. When the owl shows up in your life, it is wise to look for the signs that are guiding you to change in some way or another. Throughout our two-year relationship, Doug and I experienced a lot of changes. After we parted, we both continued to make changes in our lives and move in the direction we felt we needed to go. Reflecting, we were much more alike than we thought we were different, as we were like the spirit of the owl: always welcoming change and challenge.

Shocking news came through the telephone when I was informed of the sudden passing of both Doug and Bowie in September 2021. I am still flooded with emotions and feelings that I may never recover from as we shared so much together. Doug and Bowie sadly crashed into a tree on the Taconic Parkway in Kent, an area of Carmel, New York, during rush hour the morning after Labor Day. Doug was a gearhead, as people would say. He could fix anything, especially cars and motorcycles. He was a car racer, like my dad. He used to race dragsters at Englishtown Raceway at one point in his life. That morning, he was in the truck that I bought when Doug introduced me to pickup trucks. Doug taught me a lot about vehicles but emphasized why you should know why you love a vehicle. When we parted, he bought it off me as he loved the early-style Tacomas and how they were specifically made. One of my close friends, John Gravenese, made me a handcrafted white wooden cross that I mounted on the tree in their remembrance. Oddly enough, this was the same exit and area we had searched for homes at one point in our relationship.

Just past his accident area is a large rock, and in the middle of the rock is a thin white wooden cross. We drove past this area hundreds of times together. Doug knew I had spoken of authoring a book on "roadside memorials" at one point since there are many differences and allowances for dedications from state to state.

From time to time, we would pass the large rock, and Doug would point it out and say, "Guess he didn't make it." That was Doug, plain and simple; he had his own way of expressing things. I reflect on the elevator at the hospital and hearing the staff member call out to a coworker named Glenn. Yes, he always had his own ideas about things, but I saw him change his mind on things too. I am truly of the belief that he had a better understanding of the afterlife than he may have publicly admitted.

The day after I hung the white cross on the tree on the Taconic, I was in Yonkers at the Ridge Hill Shopping Plaza. I felt like I was in a fog and just needed a distraction. I stepped into Clark's shoe store. I had never been to this shop but was familiar with their footwear since I had bought a few boots online through Amazon. As I started to speak to the salesperson, a husky dog came up to me. Yes, in the shoe store. I blurted out, "That is a husky dog."

A male salesperson came over and apologized, explaining the dog came from the back room. I had tears in my eyes. The man said, "Did he scare you?"

I said, "No, but our husky just died recently."

This dog, just like Bowie, rubbed against my leg, licked my hand, and trotted away with the clerk. I sat there snapping photos of the dog with my cell phone with the shoes in the background. I sat there for a minute, and under my breath, I said, "Thank you." That was my sign that Doug and Bowie knew I had put up the white cross for them. As many times as I would excitedly tell Doug about the signs I was getting, dreams I was having, or even the signs I wrote about in *Seeing More than Clouds in Your Coffee*, now here he was sending me a sign from them both. This experience brought me out of my fog and gave me a feeling of peace. Some people make an imprint on your life and heart, and they did both for me.

Clay Lomakayu Miller and his wolf dog helpers

My dear friend and Mama, Reverend Lori Bruno, owner of Magika and founder of Our Lord and Lady of Trinacrian Rose Church Salem, Massachusetts

Dr. Leo Louis Martello (RIP)

Doug Day (RIP) and me at Rye Beach Playland in the winter

Doug Day and Bowie (RIP)

Bowie in our 1977 VW Bug -- he loved that car, so did Doug!

Doug Day (RIP) in the studio

Doug Day and me on the Hudson River in Dobbs Ferry, NY

Bowie's eyes

Wooden cross made by my friend John Gravenese, so I could place in their honor 2021

On their one-year anniversary, I placed two red heart balloons on the cross 2022 Carmel, Kent, New York

The husky dog in the Clark's shoe store in Ridge Hill, Yonkers NY 2021

Doug and Bowie on the East River, NYC

Chapter 6

A few years ago, someone informed me that I could take more educational courses since there was money left over in my Post-9/11 GI Bill. Returning to school was the last thing on my mind at that point, but the person suggested it could be one last educational challenge. I signed up for massage therapy. At the time, I was working and living in the Maryland-Virginia area for the National Institutes of Health and decided that taking these courses would be beneficial to my overall interest in healing arts.

Soon after signing up for these courses, I realized I was the oldest student in the class. I was in my early fifties, and I immediately thought of bailing out. Studying at an older age would be harder, and I was not sure what I would do with this possible new craft in life. Once one of the instructors heard I wanted to bail out, she leaped into action and said she refused my request to withdraw. She heard me out and said she understood all my concerns but said she would not let me give up on myself. I asked her to repeat the sentence and she did. She explained further by saying, "For all you have been through in life—in Iraq and in nursing—you are going to let massage school rock your world?" This was her message to me. She was right; I could do this one last educational challenge, I thought.

Over the years, I had taken many mini-massage and healing classes, which focused on reiki and energy, but nothing ever this formal. I trusted her and continued with the coursework. After six long months, I graduated alongside my fellow students and proudly passed the Virginia state boards for massage therapy. I was not sure how I would use this degree, but I was glad I stayed the course and saw it through to the end. I learned a lot in the massage classes, which were reminiscent of my nursing courses. Being an older student, learning was a challenge. The lesson I learned was not to give up on myself. Things that are too easy usually do not show we the true lesson. How many lessons can we really learn in our lives? How many challenges can we give ourselves? Do we really want those challenges, or do we need those challenges to learn those lessons? The answers to those questions are unknown. It is through self-reflection that we learn the answers. We often look back in life and realize why those challenges occurred and how we learned those lessons. I have had many conversations with people about the challenges they have endured. Throughout many of those challenges, lessons are learned no matter what the challenge is. Challenges can involve anything: family, work, health, and finances.

I often think of how spoiled we are to live in the United States and have so many choices, freedoms, and amenities. Traveling in the Middle East, I witnessed so many different challenges that people endure. I have seen some of the humblest people show their grateful hearts in so many caring ways. The COVID-19 pandemic challenged people throughout the world. The world endured the pandemic collectively. The idea of isolation was new to us, and the disruption of daily life impacted the total population.

At the beginning of the pandemic, little was known about the virus and its long-term effects. Individuals around the world learned about the virus through scientists, politicians, and the media. The concept of total health, including physical and mental health, became apparent and of utmost importance. Travel was becoming impossible, and industries had to change how they did business in all areas. Many of my friends in the music industry stopped touring and found themselves in their studios at home. Every line of work and every life was affected by this pandemic. With drastic changes happening on a minute-by-minute, hour-by-hour basis, it was hard for the population to predict the short-term and long-term effects on how they should be living.

For most of society, isolation is hard and often not a choice many would select. Isolation demands self-reflection and sometimes self-correction. For those who live a solo life, the pandemic took on a different view for them. Living alone, as I do, the isolation was not as impactful, but the feeling of fear of the unknown seemed greater. In the beginning weeks of COVID-19, I had been staying in a hotel since my kitchen was being renovated. Sitting in the hotel lobby watching the news unfold seemed so surreal. The hotel was in the middle of a shopping mall in Westchester County—the same shopping mall I took the bus to as a teenager. As teenagers, we would escape to the mall and shop, check out boys, and even secretly wear makeup to look older.

Those were the days, I thought, as the pandemic warning scrolled across the bottom of the TV screen. My good friend Rob Caggiano phoned to tell me he was staying in New York City, and we discussed the situation. The mayor was shutting down New York City, and he wanted to get out before that happened. I told him where I was staying, and he said he would take a room in the hotel as well. Rob and I had been through tough times before. He is the type of person who seeks knowledge and all the latest available information.

We decided to meet each evening in the lobby for updates on the pandemic. This often occurred while we sat at the bar trying to distract each other with memories of the past or songs and music conversations. He intuitively knew this was life-changing. He knew his touring and travel would stop.

Looking back, Rob and I remember those early days of confusion. The feeling of trying hard to piece together all the information as it was unfolding before our eyes seems like a distant memory now. Reflecting now, we remember the one night at the bar in the hotel lobby when we were looking up at the television and the bar server asked us what we would like to drink. Rob said, "What kind of wine do you have?"

The bar server started to name a few, and he asked her what her name was. She replied, "Evelyn."

He said, "Really? We have a song named 'Evelyn.'" She looked confused, so he pulled out his phone and played a bit of "Evelyn" by his band Volbeat. Her face lit up and she smiled. For those few minutes, all three of us had forgotten about the pandemic, and we were just enjoying the song and the name similarity. Today, that memory makes me smile as it represents living. This was early in the pandemic. We had no idea of the upcoming stress, tragedy, and sadness that would come our way. We were like many others that night who felt the confusion, frustration, and fear the virus had caused.

Within the week, I was able to return to my small studio apartment. This apartment now seemed instantly smaller as I was spending much more time in the five hundred-square-foot area. During the first months of COVID, my father's Siamese cat Tessa passed away from a leg sarcoma, and I was heartbroken. A good friend of mine took me to an animal shelter in Westchester County, where I adopted Ms. Meg Ryan, a pastel calico who was about ten years old. Meg's story was slightly shady, and her family had dropped her off for unknown reasons. I immediately understood the family had some stressors related to COVID-19. Once Meg assumed residence in my five-hundred-square-foot studio, my isolation seemed more bearable as she filled the gap that Tessa's loss created.

The animal shelters were booming, as many families sought out companionship during this dark period of isolation. When I was applying to adopt, the restrictions were tight and appointments were few, so finding Ms. Meg was meant to be, in my opinion. It has been over a year since Meg and I have been together, and we have equally endured several health challenges. Meg had a stroke while I was away during my last job with the army before my retirement. She was in a high-end cat hotel, and they cared for her with complete precision and love. This medical emergency has left her blind, which was a new challenge for both of us. Nevertheless, everyone who meets her in the apartment cannot believe she is blind. She follows me around, jumps up and down on furniture, and goes out to the hallways for her daily exercise. It is amazing to me, but according to the veterinarian, losing a sense increases all the other senses so her new challenge is no longer such a challenge.

Throughout the pandemic, the high-risk population of people who struggle with a known medical condition felt feelings of fear and uncertainty. I was among this population as I have asthma connected to my service in Southwest Asia from the burn pits. I have followed every precaution, taken all the vaccines and boosters, and have carved out a way of living in this different world. Being in this high-risk community, it is a daily effort to reassure myself that all will be fine. I had to take charge of the only thing I could control: myself.

I often reflect on the dark early days of the pandemic. Like many apartment buildings in New York City, my apartment building in Westchester County honored the health care workers every evening at 7:00 p.m. Most opened their windows and banged pots and pans and hollered out their windows, "Thank you!" Our building even played the famous song by the Beatles "Here Comes the Sun" on a loudspeaker. To this day, when I hear that song, I tear up. I live one block away from a community hospital that was hit hard with COVID-19. The "window effect," as I have called it, lasted from March to June 1. It was ninety days. No matter the weather or the day, it became a growing ritual for us to give our echoing gratitude to those health care workers at the bedsides.

In early June, when the window effect ceased, it seemed oddly quiet. We welcomed the sound of stillness as it meant less death, less fear, and eventually more freedom. So many of us were considered essential workers. Several friends, family members, and I all work in health care, and I have close friends working in the police force, firefighters, and even in the funeral industry. These essential workers were impacted and challenged daily. The ebb and flow of the virus has shown the population the concept of the unknown. We somehow always want to look ahead to see what the future will look like when it gets here. Most of the challenges that people have experienced since the beginning of the pandemic are still lingering in their lives, especially the financial and mental health challenges. It has felt like a Ferris wheel ride that you cannot exit, or like a dream that will not end. These are comments I have heard regarding the virus and the current situation.

COVID-19 has changed many lives and taken many lives. Like many of you reading, I have lost several people due to the pandemic, and this type of loss is incredibly hard. As the months continue, advances are made and vaccines are available, but the facts are still changing. It is too soon to see what the long-term effects of the virus will be globally, but these challenges will soon prove lessons for us in the future. No matter what life unfolds in your path, no matter the challenges you face, the key is not to quit. We must support and love one another, and like the instructor at the Virginia massage school, we must tell one another that we will not let others give up on themselves. By living months in isolation, perhaps we will learn to live with a bit more compassion, humanity, and forgiveness. Let the pandemic mark time and history, but let it not mark us, for we can accept any challenge thrown our way, if not alone then together.

In my mediumship readings during the pandemic, I have seen COVID-19 differently from the other side. I can only share my experiences with you, as every medium works differently. Loved ones in spirit have described their COVID passings to be respiratory related; others have described it as feeling very sleepy, and a few having experienced it as being "hit with something," describing it as a trauma. Working as a clairvoyant and clairaudient medium, I share what I am shown and explain what I hear in the readings.

In years of readings, this is the first time I have seemed to notice something different with spirit. Since COVID, messages from spirit seem to be reflections on distant memories paired with specific messages to loved ones; some messages reflect on earlier issues in relationships. Messages of love highlight the meanings of the relationships, the gratitude for the caregiving, and the understanding for the separation. There is an awareness of family members not being able to be there or not being able to do certain things. The messages address more than the grief, and often involve what families have been faced with during the trying times of COVID-19. The feelings of separation, the lockdowns, and the restrictions have been woven into the grief, and this all needs proper processing.

As I tell all my clients, one session with a medium should never take the place of proper grief work. A medium can provide evidence of spirit and can help the client understand the afterlife, but it can never provide the level of therapy that many individuals need for processing grief. COVID-19 did not discriminate in taking our loved ones. The ages and circumstances varied. Many of the deaths that occurred during COVID-19 were attributed to COVID-19 although there was another primary cause of death. This fact has caused much frustration for families. The medical effects of COVID-19 have impacted our population, but it is important to remember the many layers of grief that it has created as well.

Chapter 7

Those of you who grew up on music and adored watching live music understand the feeling music gives you. Very often after seeing a live show and then hearing those songs on the radio, you realize they are the same songs, but the experience is not. Live performers often tell stories about the lyrics or how the song came about before they perform it. Throughout the years, I have seen this done, and it is one of my favorite times during a live show. Knowing the back story often gives the song a deeper meaning or makes the lyrics come alive in a whole unusual way. Recently, I saw a performer on stage tell a story about his life and reference the concept of choices and consequences. His personal story struck a chord in me, especially after the recent experience with the global COVID-19 pandemic. Everybody has been affected by COVID-19 in some way or another. Like many others, I experienced many changes due to my own personal choices and, in turn, experienced consequences. COVID-19 made people reorganize their lives, even change their priorities, and create innovative ideas for the new lives they were living.

Sometimes songs take on a back story all on their own, especially when that song or songs hold a particular association with a time and place in your life. When I first got to Iraq, some of the soldiers I traveled with were separated into different duty assignments and locations. I started the "song of the day," which would be sent in a group email to them daily, if possible. In 2004, emails were our only type of communication with one another. The concept of the song of the day was to assign a known song to an event that occurred that day. The rules were simple, and creativity was an encouraging plus!

After explaining the concept, it caught on quickly, and our small group grew throughout time through word of mouth. A few chosen songs were "You Dropped a Bomb on Me" by the Gap Band (1982), "Welcome to the Jungle" by Guns 'n' Roses (1987), and "Gimme Shelter" by the Rolling Stones (1969). I once got off a Blackhawk helicopter, and as I was walking across the tarmac, someone pointed at me and said, "Song of the day."

I replied over the loud sound of the chopper with a thumbs-up and, "Right on!" I was more shocked that I was recognized in my complete battle rattle than that the concept that the song of the day had caught on. This is no different from the way many of you remember life events through songs. As you read this, I am sure certain songs that highlighted events in your life come to mind.

Those of you who remember dancing in the living room to your favorite albums or jamming in your garages with your friends, trying to form a local band, can smile at the overall concept of music. Does music help make the world go around, solve many of life's problems, or play a part in changing situations? My answer, personally, would be yes! Throughout the pandemic, my friend Frank Pallett had to shut down his businesses, the Chance Theater in Poughkeepsie, New York and his local gym. Like many businesses experienced, the pandemic created new changes that were not anticipated. The Chance has been a staple in our music community for many years, and I have mentioned the psychic work I have done there over the years in my first book *Seeing More than Clouds in Your Coffee*. Both Frank and his sister Carolyn Pallett Brophy were featured in that book as they were big supporters of my psychic and paranormal work. Frank had invited me over the years to attend many events at the theater that featured my psychic and paranormal skills. One of his invitations included me being the guest psychic medium for a reality show they made at the Chance Theater called *Between a Rock and a Hard Place*. *Between a Rock and a Hard Place* was directed by Daniel Bucci. The reality show was featured at the Tribeca Film Festival but was unsuccessful. However, I understand it was successful at the film festival in California.

As the pandemic news began to spread along with the virus, Frank did not have a choice but to close his businesses. Frank kept us connected by recording a weekly radio show called *Live at the Chance* on Z93, which I listened to through the iHeart radio app on Saturday evenings. He and his sister Carolyn sat side by side during the show as co-hosts, weaving in songs and stories of the bands who have played throughout the years at the Chance. During the week, their Facebook page offered a chance for listeners to request a song or band to be played during the show. I often wrote in, requesting my favorite song "Rainbow in the Dark" by Dio, or Carolyn would play a Volbeat song for me since she knew I was friends with Rob Caggiano.

One night, Frank and Carolyn surprised me while I was home listening to the prerecorded show. They mentioned me by rank for my military service and being a first responder during COVID-19. In 2020, I was expected to retire from the United States Army Reserve. However, due to the pandemic, I extended my retirement for an additional year to assist the division for which I was working. As they mentioned me, I began to smile since they were always cheering me on throughout the years, supporting every effort, event, or job I set out to do. Throughout my psychic, military, or even motorcycle charity work, they were always there to support me and spread the word. Turning off the radio that evening, I reflected on my years of friendship with them both. I thought of them amid the confusing pandemic and the economic impact Frank had felt. These friends of mine were siblings, and together through their creativity they found a way to keep the Chance family together. Frank was always known for giving unknown bands a chance at the Chance. He was always striving for perfection in his work and making a difference in people's lives. Many friends over the years met at the Chance and made memories there that will live on forever. Going to sleep that night, I looked forward to seeing the Chance reopen in July 2021 and putting this pandemic in our past.

The Chance finally had its opening day in July of 2021, but the opening was tangled in a web of tragic events which quickly unfolded. Just prior to the opening of the Chance, we lost Bob Morf, the production manager, in a sudden tragic motorcycle accident. The week of opening night, Frank had a sudden medical condition that led to hospitalization; sadly, he did not survive. Just two months later, we unexpectedly lost his sister Carolyn to a medical condition as well. These shocking, devastating passings of friends who were parents were unimaginable to all of us. Our music community was devastated and in complete disbelief. The lyrics of my always requested song by Dio echoed in my mind: "When there's lightning, you know it always brings me down, / 'Cause it's free and I see that's it's me, / who's lost and never found." The song is about depression, and we were all feeling it.

Just recently, I attended a Dokken reunion show with George Lynch and Don Dokken at the Chance. Looking at the sea of attendees, I knew why they were all there. It was not just to see the band but also to witness what Frank made during the pandemic. He perfected the sound and lighting system and made many efforts to create a total experience for the attendees. That night, we could feel the energy of the crowd and hear the power of the music. The roar of the crowd and cheers were directed straight to the afterlife. Many of us commented that we felt all of them there that night with us. The energy of the Chance was electrifying and filled with love. There are few men like Frank Pallett, in my opinion. For those of us who have had the pleasure of knowing him, our lives were altered in some intrinsic way and for that we thank him.

Frank Pallett's band Big Guns has a song, "Life Goes On," which is the third track on the record entitled *Re-Loaded*, released in March 2017. This is a well-known song that was often played on the program *Live from the Chance* on Z93. The song is dedicated to Frank's friend Mike who passed tragically many decades earlier. The chorus words are "can't you see life goes on, / don't forget me now that I'm gone, / every day you're on my mind, / can't you see that life goes on." One of the best versions of this song is found on YouTube where the band plays with musician guest singer Ms. Rachel Lorin. Now that we have lost both Frank and his sister Carolyn, this song has developed an even bigger meaning for many of us.

My best buddy Rob Caggiano, lead guitarist for Volbeat, formerly lead guitarist for Anthrax and is a five-time GRAMMY nominated record producer. Photo taken in Dobbs Ferry NY during the Covid-19 pandemic (2020)

My cat Meg Ryan believes in always keeping calm and doing her meditation

Meg Ryan is always such a fashionista

Meg Ryan and me celebrating St. Patrick's Day 2022

Bob Morf (RIP) US Air Force Veteran (1971-1974) and production manager at The Chance

Frank Pallett (RIP) and Carolyn Pallett Brophy (RIP)

Carolyn Pallett Brophy (RIP) "Live from the Chance" radio show

Dokken hits the stage at The Chance 12/11/2021

Frank Pallett (RIP) owner of The Chance with Nikki Johannessen who is currently managing the Chance since Frank has entered the afterlife

Chapter 8

Throughout the years, I have found it sometimes tough to be me. Many of my friends understand my psychic abilities, but meeting new people sometimes is not as easy. Just after Hurricane Sandy, New York City was rebuilding and recovering from the damage and destruction. Our roadways and some buildings took a beating as massive water came onto our shoreline, especially in Lower Manhattan. City workers were all over the city, either fixing electricity, doing construction, or just rebuilding.

My friend said she wanted to introduce me to a city worker since she loved the idea of matchmaking. I never liked blind dates, but I thought I would make her happy. My friend was always looking out for me in the dating department and thought this guy would be the perfect match. She showed me his photo and told me he was extremely interested in meeting me. The only catch was that I would have to be flexible in meetings since they were working a lot of overtime.

To not get my hopes up, I suggested meeting him during a coffee break so that within the first few minutes, we could figure it out if we really needed to pursue a formal date. He agreed, so after work one evening, I walked across town to the grid coordinates I was given and did not see him. I checked the time and looked around. I stood there and then I heard, "Hey, hey" coming from behind me. I spun around and saw the city worker. He smiled; he was wearing a yellow rain slicker over his overalls, and appeared to have a hard hat under his arm. He looked like he belonged in a hunky calendar.

He immediately said, "Let's take a walk" and told me his name. He knew the area well and explained that if we walked around the block, by the time we returned to that spot, he could grab a slice of pizza and head back to work.

"So, this is your coffee break," I said.

He nodded. He started to discuss his work and what assignments they had been getting since the hurricane occurred. I filled him in on a few fun facts about me and then told him about my book and work as a psychic medium. He stared at me a lot. I kept looking away and then back. I asked him if he had a problem with that. He explained he had never met someone like me but was a good judge of character and he felt that he should have been a cop. At that point, he grabbed my arm and walked me into an alcove of a fancy office building. I did not know what to expect, and then I realized he had brought me in there to show me a beautiful sculptured fountain waterfall. Looking down, I saw so many pennies in the bottom of the fountain and commented on it. "Wishes—I love making wishes," he said.

I said, "Okay, so we can make one." I reached into my pocket and held out two pennies, one old and one new. "Which one do you want?" I asked. He took off his gloves and picked the fresh penny. He counted to three, and we tossed them in. He smiled at me so brightly, like he was six years old all over again. We continued our walk around the block, and he commented on how easy it was to speak with me. He also mentioned that he was surprised he was having fun. He further explained that he meets so many women and many of them are just not right for him.

"Here it is," he said and stepped into Ray's pizzeria. He held up his money and two fingers, which signaled to the pizza boy to give him two slices.

"You sure you don't want anything?" he asked, stacking the slices one on top of the other.

I smiled and said, "No, thank you."

He was shoveling the stacked slices into his mouth, and he shook his head from the heat of them. Once he swallowed, he grabbed my arm and pointed to the ground—two pennies, one bright and one darker. "Holy," he said. "That's creepy."

"Okay, two pennies," I said.

"Oh no, like our wishes. Does that mean they will come true?" he asked.

I said, "Only time will tell."

He started to look at me differently, like he was spooked. Walking down the street, he was still shoveling in his stacked slices but in silence. I asked him what the best part of the walk was. He looked at me and said, "Meeting you." I smiled. His buddies were hollering at him by his last name as he threw on his hard hat, winked, and ran across the street.

My friend called a few days later and said he would like to ask for another date. I had mixed feelings about it and told her about the pennies and the wishes. She laughed and encouraged another meeting. We arranged to meet the following week at a well-known bar in town. It was around Valentine's Day, so the place was filled with red hearts and cupid signs. Waiting for him at the table seemed awkward with all these love decorations surrounding me. I tried to remain hopeful, but deep down inside, I knew the only hearts dancing around would be the decorations.

He appeared and we ordered a drink. Throughout our conversation, which was based mostly on his overtime and work, he slipped a few questions about my work as a psychic, and I sensed I was not for him. I thought I was right again and wondered why I bothered to even date anyone. Then I realized why I did when he admitted he really enjoyed making that wish, and added he got his promotion a couple of days before. It was the promotion he wished for, he admitted. I smiled. He asked me what my wish was, and I said, "Mine came true also."

"Really, what was it?" he asked.

I said, "A second date with you."

He smiled, but when the check arrived, he said, "I think it's best we just say it was real." This was his way of telling me he was not interested in another date.

I said, "That's right, it was real magic." And he smiled.

What is magic, you might ask. What isn't it, I say. I have so many magical stories to share with you. Growing up in the1970s, you could not turn on the TV set without seeing a magic show or magic referenced in some form or another. This was the time of many great magicians, such as David Copperfield, Doug Henning, Siegfried and Roy, and even Penn and Teller. You might be asking yourself when you remembered seeing magic for the first time. Was it onstage, in person, or just on television? Watching magic is intriguing; every trick seems more amazing.

In the early 1970s, my sister and I watched a wonderful children's show called *The Magic Garden*, which was produced locally by WPIX-11 in New York City. It featured Ms. Paula Janis and Ms. Carole Demas. The singing twosome brought joy to many children with stories, songs, and jokes. The set was colorful and had a Magic Tree that lowered lollipop sticks, and a garden of daisies referred to as the Chuckle Patch. The Chuckle Patch had jokes hidden inside, and after the twosome told the jokes to the children, the daisies would giggle. I must admit this was my favorite part of the show. The tree and the daisies were featured spots in the show. They helped express happiness, fun, and laughter along with the imaginary idea that the tree and flowers were participating. These two singers had it right: when you are a child, you need an escape or someone to take you on an unbelievable journey that only a child could appreciate. To us, there was no better place for that but in the Magic Garden. The singers would always end the show, singing the song "See Ya." The song had a memorable tune, the lyrics wished us well, and set the intention to see us again.

I never learned to do magic tricks. I never had a desire to learn them. Some things happened in my life that seemed magical, but they were never tied to any magical tricks. The magic I make is made through intentions, like wishes. My father and I spoke about magic a lot, especially when he would catch something on TV or hear a story on the radio station talk show *Coast to Coast AM* with the late Art Bell and George Noory. *Coast to Coast AM* is a program that airs while most people are sleeping. Throughout the years, Dad struggled with a few medical conditions and found sleep a challenge at times. Dad was very curious about the guests that George would select to interview and often took notes to remember when the daylight hours hit. I remember when I told Dad that I was deciding to attend Arthur Findlay College for psychic studies. He listened closely and then agreed. He shared with me a fact that I did not know. Dad had an enthusiasm for Houdini.

During the conversation, I was instantly taken aback by the number of facts Dad knew about Houdini's life, magic, and death. Dad quickly reminded me that there were two great feature films made on his life. One film was *Houdini* (1953), which was directed by George Marshall and starred Tony Curtis and Janet Leigh; the other was a made-for-TV movie, *The Great Houdini* (1976), directed by Melville Shavelson and starring Paul Michael Glaser and Sally Struthers. Dad also mentioned a wonderful article on Houdini that was published by *Reader's Digest* magazine, where Dad had worked for twenty-five years. The article is in the July 1981 edition and is called "Death and Magician: The Mystery of Houdini."

Harry Houdini was born in 1874 in Budapest, Hungary, and died on Halloween in 1926 in Detroit, Michigan. His partner and wife Bess lived until 1943. Dad spoke of sharing the same healthy skepticism as Houdini regarding mediums. He spoke in detail about how Houdini was caught off guard that Halloween night and received several abdominal blows, which landed him in the hospital and led to his sudden death. When Dad spoke of me attending Arthur Findlay College, he expressed its importance since readings need to be conducted with pure details that no one would know. He mentioned the word *charlatans* and discussed the reputation of these fake psychics. He told me that Houdini had given his wife a secret code so she would know he was communicating with her from the afterlife. The code was "Rosabelle answer tell pray answer look tell answer answer tell." *Rosabelle* had been inscribed in her wedding band and reflected the song she sang when she and Houdini met. Apparently, each word or pair of words represents a letter, and the combination of words represents and spells out the word *believe*. There was much controversy over whether Arthur Ford truly relayed the code to Bess during a séance in 1929. However, it is a known fact that he never claimed the reward of $10,000. Bess had made a public statement that she would award anyone who could produce a worthy message with the code from her late husband. Dad was fascinated by magic and the life of Houdini. Houdini's life was filled with making great escapes happen through magic, and years after his death, he still leaves us wondering.

Thinking back now, I can see why dad loved magic: his dad did it. When I was growing up, I was introduced to magic by my grandfather. We called him Nornie, which means grandpa. He did not speak English, only Spanish. He would communicate with us kids by showing us different magic tricks. He was highly creative and knew many complex tricks. I was the baby of the bunch, so I was the first to give up trying to figure out a trick and sat on the sidelines watching my cousins make multiple attempts to sort it out.

Nornie also made us handcrafted jewelry. The jewelry was made from watermelon and cantaloupe seeds. Now that to me was real magic. I once remember asking my nana where these necklaces and bracelets came from, and she mentioned he made them by hand. I was blown away since they were so beautiful. He sorted, washed, and dried the seeds on the windowsill on paper towels in their Brooklyn apartment. Once they were good and dry, Nornie would score the seeds with a pen, make a hole with a sewing needle, and thread them together.

When we visited, the final pieces were laid on the table for our choosing. I felt like I had entered Tiffany's and was peering into a display cabinet of diamonds. Nornie became creative with his designs, and he started to mix and match the seeds, making each item original and different. Each bracelet or necklace would have a unique design of mixed seeds. Clearly, he thought out each piece with care. My cousins and I would select our set, usually a necklace and bracelet, and he would put them on us. We would eagerly run to the mirror to see his fashion and true magic. To this day, my cousins and I laugh, remembering turning our heads in the slightest way and feeling the pang or pinch of a cantaloupe seed in our neck. They did not last over time, but his magic and those stories have lasted a lifetime.

Magic has always been fascinating to people. Watching a card or coin trick, or even watching a levitation act, leaves an audience in wonderment. You might ask what the attraction is or why people are fascinated by the imagination, illumination, or process. Perhaps it is because a magic trick cannot be explained logically. When I watched Nornie, I would ask for the method of the trick. As my cousins would explain, no good magician ever gives the secrets of the tricks away. The concept of revealing the trick, answer, or reason somehow takes the same magic away.

Harry Houdini (RIP) escape artist, illusionist, stunt performer

Houdini with his mother Cecilia Weisz (RIP) and wife Bess (RIP)

My Nornie (RIP)

Nornie's hand crafted jewelry made of cantaloupe seeds

Dad with his parents in their garden after they relocated from Brooklyn to New Jersey

The 1980s were filled with fashion and fun and my best friends like Cookie and Dave White...Dave and I were always hanging out in Yonkers or going to Washington Square Park, finding a street fair and sitting on his roof top...listening to heavy metal and creating our dreams. He is living the dream in Las Vegas with his family.

In 2013 I got involved in supporting motorcycle charity work for wounded combat Veterans, in particular helping my cousin Andrew Biggio (USMC Veteran Iraq/Afghanistan) with the Boston Wounded Vet Run and running two New York Wounded Vet Runs (2014 and 2015)

Me in the late 1980's big hair and the fashion

Dave White and me

Boston Wounded Vet Run with my cousin and Founder Andy Biggio

Sniper Georgi Ruley's photos

New York Wounded Vet Run

Boston Wounded Vet Run - Rick Wood (RIP)

Phoenix Wounded Vet Run

Cathy playing dress up

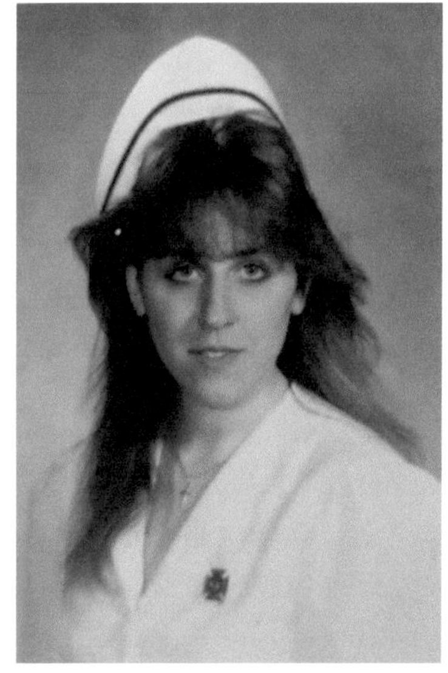

Cathy graduated Cochran School of Nursing 1989

Cathy working in Salem, Massachusetts

Cathy

Chapter 9

It was the late 1970s when Mr. Chuck Mangione played his flugelhorn in one of his great hit singles, "Feels So Good." I am sure many of you will remember the song. Decades later, it was this song that brought me back to 1979 and a visit to my aunt Helen (my mother's favorite cousin) and her husband Jack in Manchester, Vermont. Helen had recently retired from years of working at AT&T, and they had selected a newly built condominium called Murray Hill to make their new home. We were young girls around eleven or twelve, and we were so excited to see the green mountains, try the maple syrup, and attend the dinner parties. My aunt and uncle knew how to throw a party and attend a party as well. While we were there, we were given jobs servers for a fancy cocktail party at the condominium of my aunt's neighbor. Her neighbor had delicious appetizers, and we needed to learn how to describe them and make them sound amazing. I mastered the grape-leaf description, and the attendees thought we were just adorable. Walking through the much-taller adults and offering my appetizer tray to them, I dreamed of being an adult with the high heels and latest fashion.

As I got to my late teenage years, I would go up to Vermont and spend a week helping her with Jack. He had become much more fragile as he struggled with diabetes. He still enjoyed his hamburger at the Double Hex in town and his cigar. They let me drive their Lincoln Continental, which was a huge car for me since I was driving Dad's Plymouth Horizon around that time. Jack, who looked like a twin of George Burns, and Helen, who could have been a double for Elizabeth Taylor, made a terrific couple. Helen and Jack had their own kind of style. During my visits, they always had cocktails at 5:00 p.m., with music floating in the background. Helen would prepare dinner, so everyone was eating by 9:00 p.m. She was a fabulous cook, like my mom, and genuinely enjoyed doing it. I have great memories of ordering in restaurants in Vermont as she lovingly teased my dad about how he ordered his steak. They marveled over how my grandmother served meat almost still mooing, which always horrified my father.

Dad and Helen were very much alike and understood the business scene in New York City during the 1960s and 1970s. Jack had his own Snap-On tool business, which Dad thought was great. Helen, much like my father, enjoyed being a volunteer. Once she moved to Manchester, she became a volunteer at Hildene, which was the summer home of Robert Todd Lincoln, the son of our sixteenth president. She fell in love with Hildene and studied to become a docent. Docents are guides, who are considered subject matter experts in their fields, and work in art galleries, museums, and such. I had many conversations with her about her work as a docent when I was volunteering at the 9/11 Memorial and Museum in New York City. She was very well-liked and very well respected at Hildene and is still remembered to this day.

Once Jack died in 1992, she began to snowbird to the beach area in Indian Harbor, near Melbourne, Florida. She enjoyed missing the tough winters of Vermont as she would watch the waves roll in from her patio terrace. I often visited her there as well. She was always great fun. One year, she suggested I bring my father's sister with me. My father's sister had recently lost her husband and was alone in the New Port Richey area. I took Helen's suggestion and traveled over to the east coast of Florida with Aunt Carmen. Helen showed her around and made her feel at home. Every morning, Carmen would sit on the terrace reading her Bible and listening to the waves crashing on the shore. Helen mentioned to me that she felt that was exactly what she needed. Helen understood the loss of a spouse and understood needing solitude and a change of atmosphere. As Carmen and I returned to New Port Richey, she mentioned she felt the trip was just what she needed. Helen was right again. She could definitely read people; she knew in her heart and her eyes what someone was saying or not saying. She was filled with her own boisterous energy and gift of gab and was not afraid to speak her mind no matter the subject. She was clever and a force to be reckoned with, as some found out.

In mid-April 2019, Helen entered the afterlife after living in a lovely assisted-living facility in Manchester. She enjoyed the facility, the socialization, and the staff. Every time I visited, she reminisced of the years of long ago. She spoke so often about my mother and her family and her Jack and their Irish setter Cindi. Helen was always a spitfire and lived in good health to the age of ninety-five. Somehow, her affairs were not all in order, and sorting them became a bit complex, legally speaking. The situation seemed more than confusing and frustrating, and I was not a main player in the discussion.

As 2022 rolled around, I decided to reach out and take the monetary responsibility for burying her. When I contacted the funeral parlor and cemetery, everything seemed to come together quickly. The following day, after making all the needed phone calls, I was walking in my neighborhood to find where I parked my car. I looked up, and there was a woman walking her Irish setter. My mouth dropped open, and I whispered,

"Cindi." Later that day, I was leaving my bank in town. I smelled the strongest smell of cigar smoke. I walked around my car, looked around at other vehicles, and even went over to the sidewalk; no one smoking was in sight. I whispered, "Uncle Jack." I knew these signs were all for me and my upcoming trip to bury Helen.

It was a Friday night. As I drove onto Route 7 headed toward Manchester, the sky was uniquely colored yellow and black, appearing to seem like the night was taking over the day. It was dramatic and movie-like, and I whispered, "I am here, Aunt Helen." Farther on, as I passed a few exits, I experienced heavy snow, which was unexpected and was not in the forecast. Over the years, Helen had told me many snow stories, including heroic stories of her driving "white-knuckled" during snow in Manchester.

When I got to the motel where I was staying, the woman at the desk asked why I was in town. Through small talk, I told her about my aunt. It being a small town, she mentioned that her parents knew Helen. I added, "Of course they would, as she always drove around with her vanity license plates that read HHH30: Helen Hansen Hurley and the 30 was for her condominium number." The clerk told me to drive down to the gas station at the bottom of the hill for snacks since I had arrived late. As I was walking out of the gas station shop, a car pulled up, and a young girl got out. Her license plate was HHE330. I took a picture, got back into my vehicle, and whispered, "Okay, Helen, you know I am here."

The following day, I picked up her ashes at the funeral parlor and took her for her last ride through Hildene, the place where she had spent so much time and made so many memories. It was far more relevant to me than to drive her through her condominium complex. Hildene was magical for her; it connected her with the town and community she grew to love. My next stop was her final resting place which was right next to Hildene—a quaint old cemetery called Dellwood. It is surprisingly huge. I met up with the caretaker, and he graciously gave me some privacy for my final goodbye. I read two prayers, Psalms 23, and John 5:24, and played Benny Goodman's "In the Mood." As it played, I danced my best version of solo swing dance on the grave. As I spun around, I saw the caretaker in the distance staring and probably wondering what the heck was I doing. As I finished, I told them I loved them and thanked them for being in my life. As I waved the caretaker over, we shared some stories, and he remembered Helen.

He said, "Didn't she drive a Cutlass?"

I said, "She sure did, and it was a convertible."

He said, smiling, "Yes, you are right."

I laid beautiful fresh flowers, a mixture I bought at the food mart across from her assisted-living facility; it was the same food mart where I had bought her flowers during those previous visits. I made sure to include three white Easter lilies and a rose, all symbolic to me of peace and love.

Later that afternoon, after the burial, I drove to the condominium complex, drove through the south section where I once owned a condominium, and then through the Heights section where number 30 is located. I stopped briefly and reflected on so many memories from visiting Helen with Mom and Dad. Then I started to drive down the hill to leave. The song on the radio, "You're So Vain" by Carly Simon, caught my attention. This is the song with the famous phrase "clouds in my coffee," which inspired me to title my first book *Seeing More than Clouds in Your Coffee*. Instantly, I knew I needed to add Helen's story to this book. The song was a sign of thanks and acknowledgment of knowing I brought her to her final resting place as she so desired in life.

I often say to myself what I remember most about someone when he or she enters the afterlife. With Helen, there are too many things to list. That's when you know that person mattered in your life, and you mattered to them. When the movie *Oh God* featuring George Burns and John Denver came out in 1977, everyone was abuzz since it was a phenomenal movie about belief. We were thrilled since Uncle Jack reminded us so much of George, just taller and lankier. The entire movie is great; my favorite part is at the end, when Denver's character hears that Burns' character is leaving and asks him, "Sometimes, now, and then, couldn't we just talk?"

George Burns's character, God, responds, saying, "I'll tell you what. You talk, I'll listen." And he walks out into the horizon. This scene is about talking to God, but to me is very much like talking to those we love in the afterlife. We talk and they listen.

My Aunt Helen Hurley (RIP)

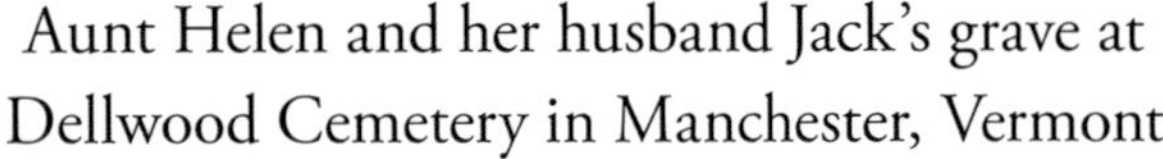

Aunt Helen and her husband Jack's grave at Dellwood Cemetery in Manchester, Vermont

Robert Todd Lincoln's Hildene home in Manchester, Vermont

Murray Hill Condominium Manchester Center, Vermont

Chapter 10

In the late 1990s, I was working for a health insurance company as a registered nurse when my father's health started to change. My dad faced a tough time as his doctors were suggesting he had a cancer diagnosis different from his previous cancer. I desperately needed to get him back to Memorial Sloan Kettering (MSK) in New York City. However, the doctor he needed had an extraordinarily long wait list. I began to worry. I spoke to a colleague about my situation. He suggested I speak with our medical director about the situation. I was afraid, but I did not have any choice, I thought. I was more than surprised to find out that our medical director knew the physician, understood the urgency, and told me to call and use his name as a reference. I eagerly told Dad I was able to get this done, and our journey started. His situation was dreadful. This famous doctor explained in detail that he did not have long to decide, but he needed surgery. He explained that this surgery was so dangerous that more than 50 percent of those who have it do not survive it.

The physician said in his deep foreign accent, "Joe, whatever you want to do, do it. But if you do not have this surgery in three weeks from now, you may perish."

As we walked out of the hospital, I asked Dad what he would like to do. He said, "I will have the surgery, but after living in Brooklyn for thirty-seven years of my life, I never walked across the Brooklyn Bridge, so let's do that."

It was January, and it was only seven degrees outside. The two of us were already dressed for the winter weather, so we drove down to the bridge and walked across it. I have some wonderful photos of us with the World Trade Center Twin Towers in the distance. Dad was beaming; he thought it was great. He miraculously survived that surgery and became the most well-known patient to survive it well into the mid-2000s, when he no longer needed to check in with the MSK team. Dad often spoke about his visits to Memorial Sloan Kettering when the residents and those attending shook his hand, knowing he had been one of the rare and lucky ones. Dad got to know this famous physician well and often brought him a bottle of wine as a token of gratitude.

My coworker brought me an image on a small piece of paper and left it on my desk. It was a drawing in black and white of a coffee mug with a girl sitting in it; the cup read, "Cathy's worry cup." I smiled; he later explained by telling me about the book *Becky and the Worry Cup: A Children's Book about a Parent's Cancer*, which was published by Perennial Publishing in 1997. Although I was an adult, to my coworker, I still had a parent with cancer. Just having that piece of paper on my desk brought me a sense of calm during an incredibly stressful time. My coworker was a very insightful social worker and often found clever ways to make me smile or tease me when I feared the unknown.

As you can imagine by now, my dad was a big part of my life and was included in many of my life choices. Every time he took ill, it rocked my world. I was no different than other children as we are always trying to do our best to protect, care for, and provide for our parents. I am a big believer that we choose our parents in this lifetime, and if I am coming back, I would easily choose him again. He taught me so much in life, but he also gave me the incredible sense of the importance of giving back to others too. After he retired, he became a volunteer, and he loved it. His volunteering included working with those struggling with blindness, HIV, dementia, and veterans with spinal cord injuries.

About ten years or so ago, my father and I were leaving the local American Legion. He was a proud veteran and executive officer at the Legion. He was extremely popular and had many friends at the meetings. There were very few women veterans attending, and I sat at my dad's table at every meeting. Leaving the meeting one night, I told him I was not interested in attending any more meetings. He looked shocked and asked why. I could not relate to the stories, and no one asked me much about Iraq. He said, "Well, you can always change your table." I looked at him. "That is right," he said. "You do not have to leave. You can just change your table, and in doing that, you change the conversation."

That evening, I reflected on his advice. I had followed that same advice throughout both my civilian and military careers. When things felt stagnant or when I needed a change, I switched jobs and very often boosted my opportunity for a promotion. After he passed, it was too difficult to attend since he was so dearly missed by so many. The facility was too hard to enter because it totally represented him.

One evening, I received a phone call from my childhood friend. The voice was so familiar. He said, "Hey, Cat, it's Jim—Jim McGovern." He immediately thanked me for my service and told me about the VFW 1666 in Yonkers where he was the commander. He asked me to attend. I heard my father's voice remind me of the saying, "You can always change your table." I said yes.

Sometimes in life, especially as combat veterans, we find it hard to feel understood, especially by civilians. These days, everyone has a political opinion. Unfortunately, many of them are not informed or do not have a clue what they are talking about. If you want to change your table, change your conversation, or just get out of the house. Do it; you never know what is waiting for you out there.

Change is hard for everyone, especially if you are struggling with grief. It sometimes feels easier to do less, think more, and not get involved. Grief is a personal experience. I often reflect on a book I received in the second grade called *Chicken Little*, also known as *Henny Penny*. I was curious about the character, a chicken who believed "the sky was falling" and the world was coming to an end because an acorn had fallen on her head. I cannot tell you how many times I read the book, and I carried it around with me. The book was given to me by a classmate at my birthday party. There was something so curious to me about this nervous chicken in a state of panic. At an early age, I realized children can be like the chicken: not always understanding what was happening around them, especially with family stress. The book reminds children to have courage in the face of any situation, even when it feels like the sky is falling. Courage was the same theme in the *Captains Courageous* book Dad read to me while I was in the hospital as a child. Having courage is tough, since it exposes your vulnerabilities, but it is an admirable trait to have.

Be courageous, be brave, be kind, be loving, be understanding, be forgiving, be happy, but most of all, be you! We are all waking up and walking through this life, and we all cannot be the same or do the same things. You need to be on your journey to discover what really matters to you in life. Sometimes it takes a while to understand what is best for you. Very often in grief, it is hard to add anything else to your plate, but keep yourself open to possibilities. Perhaps you are like Helen, my dad, and me and will choose to volunteer one day. "By giving you are receiving," as Helen used to say. I wish you the best on your journey. Remember, time moves amazingly fast. Everyone you meet in life somehow offers a chance for you, either to be different, think differently, or no longer be traveling in that same direction. Stay open to dreaming as a vivid dreamer. Since I was a child, this has come easy for me, but has not for everyone, and I understand that. Many times, people ask me if we can see our loved ones in dreams, and I say yes, we can. If you do dream at night, start to jot down the details after waking, even if they do not make sense right away. You can prepare for dreaming by setting the intention and welcoming the spirit world to appear in your dreams.

One of my favorite songs of the 1970s is Gary Wright's song "Dream Weaver," a song you have heard in several movies. Gary was inspired to write this song after reading *Autobiography of a Yogi*, published in 1946, which was a book given to him by another famous musician, Mr. George Harrison. It is a well-known life-changing spiritual book. The lyrics of the Gary Wright song helps to set the intention to dream: "Ooh, dream weaver / I believe you can get me through the night."

Grief is painful. The incredible feeling of loss can paralyze and somehow suspend you for a time in your life. Even after working through grief, grief can reappear in different forms, sometimes through unrelated events, and remind us of the actual experience. Through my work as a medium and through being a sitter in medium sessions, I have been shown evidence of spirit in the afterlife. The messages and evidence are remarkable; they relay peace, love, and the reassurance of reuniting again with our loved ones in the afterlife. Look for the signs of the afterlife. They are all around us, providing us comfort at surprisingly the most perfect times.

The next time you are driving, look up to see that street sign or license plate, or hear the song on the radio. Just recently, I was driving on the Bronx River Parkway on my way to an Eagles concert. The parkway was a road my dad and I took often, and the vehicle next to me had a license plate that read, "DOLLYJJ." Dad used to call my sister and me "Dolly," and he was "Joe Jr." I smiled and looked at the empty passenger seat next to me. In the recent past, in a reading, I told a sitter of a cute nickname her father had given her. Seeing the license plate reminded me of the nickname my father had given me. These signs are for us. Not everyone will understand, believe, or agree; but remember, grief is your experience, and your loss is very personal. Every day we live, we are given a new chance as each day is truly a gift, especially in these changing times. I remember seeing a sticker on a post in a parking lot in Iraq that read, "Life is Good"—which it is! Standing there in the unbearable heat, wearing a complete battle rattle, I knew life is good because we are still here to make a difference, a concept we confronted on a daily basis in Iraq.

Search every day for the good, try to make things better, and have an influence. If you struggle with finding your direction, set the intention and stay open to opportunities that will cross your path. Sometimes in life, all we need is a gentle reminder, like iconic motivating sayings like "Life is good," "Stay gold," or "Just do it." Just remember: it is never too late to change your table, change your conversation, or change your path. Just continue being the best you can be. Life is a journey; keep discovering the unknown and take the treasure in the gifts that are put on your path.

Chapter 11

Every death is difficult, but the deaths of those who have chosen to leave this world by suicide are especially heartbreaking. My experience with suicide has been quite different than most as it has occurred throughout my path in different forms. My earliest memory of a discussion about suicide was with my father, a devout Roman Catholic. One day after mass, he spoke in detail about suicide and its effects on the family. He added his beliefs about it and the teachings of the church, but he felt very strongly about it. That conversation left an impression with me and a feeling there was more to his story that he just was not sharing.

As a young girl, I remember my mother speaking about someone she knew who was a lawyer who had committed suicide. The details seemed difficult. As a child, I imagine I just really did not understand the whole situation, but I remember her being in complete shock. As a teenager, I stayed in touch with a few of the kids who had attended the Catholic Youth Organization (CYO) weekends. I received a phone call one evening at home from one of the kids. He had sat at my table and was part of my group during the weekend. I was taken aback to hear from him and then remembered we all shared our home phone numbers. He started speaking about the weekend, reminded me about our group, and then informed me he attempted to take his own life several months after the weekend. I was speechless as I listened to his journey to recover from the injuries sustained in his attempt. I was happy to hear he was back on the basketball team at his high school and helping to win the games again. After I hung up the phone, I reflected on our conversation. Out of everyone at that CYO group table, he was the least likely, I thought, to consider taking his life. He was the star of the basketball team, he was his family's favorite, and he was handsome. *Who would have thought?* my young mind pondered.

In my early twenties, my friends the McLarnon twins lost their sister Dee-Dee to suicide, and we were all in shock. She was beautiful and so truly kind. Losing Dee-Dee was like losing a family member. We would all pal around together, and I even included her in a short film I made about the AIDS crisis for my nursing program at Mercy College. In life, she very much resembled Madonna, and I gave her the role of playing a prostitute. The film was very realistic, and while filming, we feared the girls would get pulled over by the Yonkers police. Thankfully, that never happened. The film came out great, and I received an extremely high grade for the creativity and realness of the film. Years later, that is one of the only films we have of Dee-Dee. I can still hear her laughing and saying, "Oh my God," as we replayed the film before submission.

When I first joined the military, one of the soldiers was a New York City police officer. On our lunch break, he spoke about the scene of suicide that he responded to earlier that week. His story and the details of the family with small children have stayed with me to this day.

When I was in Iraq, I remember someone informing us while we were in the chow hall that a well-respected officer, a West Point graduate, had taken his life while we were there. Hearing the news in the chow hall seemed to stop all time. However, the person followed up the conversation with a surprisingly short statement: "Don't think about it too much." This statement now, years later, seems horrid. However, we were in the middle of a combat zone, and explosions were a daily occurrence. Keeping our spirits up and chins held high was a daily chore for all of us. Knowing what was going to happen to us while we were there was the complete unknown.

Throughout my career in both nursing and the military, we have been aware of suicide and have taken numerous courses to identify it. However, within the past decade, thankfully, there has been a push to educate about suicide, to educate about the signs, symptoms, and patterns of someone struggling with various mental health conditions. The Veterans Administration has released data that reflects the sad fact that twenty-two veterans die each day by suicide. Those statistics must change, and the only way they will change is through continued awareness and support. Many people struggle with mental illness but are fearful of sharing this information due to judgment. Suicide does not discriminate. Families throughout the world have been saddened by the loss of someone through the act of suicide. The situations and people vary; no two people struggle in the same way. This is a very real fact for those who have leadership positions, are highly educated, and have achieved remarkable success in their life. One may ask, why would someone so lucky, so rich, and so successful want to end his or her life? There are many unanswered questions for those left behind, no matter how the person lived his or her life.

Over the years, I have followed the soap opera *General Hospital*; the main character Sonny Corinthos is played by the actor Maurice Benard. Maurice is the author of the *New York Times* best-selling book *Nothing General About It: How Love (and Lithium) Saved Me On and Off General Hospital.* Maurice has also started a podcast called "State of Mind with Maurice Benard" to interview others on mental health issues in a storytelling fashion. It is people like Maurice who are paving the way forward to create a discussion about mental health and illness so that families, friends, and coworkers are aware and can assist in times of need and struggle.

One of the biggest lessons I learned in the military was to always be prepared. The military teaches you to expect the unexpected and to always be ready. However, sometimes situations or jobs, like being in the military, for example, can change you or change your health. Look beneath the surface, listen with a closer ear, and see with deeper eyes when in the presence of others. The person you are with may be truly struggling, and he or she may not want anyone to know it. Trying to help someone who does not want help is beyond difficult; that I know firsthand. Ensuring the person that you are there whenever he or she needs you is key. Leave loneliness alone. That's right, I said it. I tend to be alone a lot myself, but someone truly struggling should not be alone. I have an "open-door coffee" policy. My door is always open, and my coffee is always ready. If you need me, I will be there.

“Dee-Dee” Judith Susan Goldberg,
their younger sister (RIP)

Glenn and Cliff McLarnon
“McLarnon Twins” in a band photo

Glenn McLarnon (RIP) and me on the Circle Line in NYC 1990

Glenn and Cliff McLarnon in their band "Nervous Wreck",
at the Lowdown in Mount Vernon NY

Twin Towers, from the back of the Staten Island Ferry 1998

THE BOOK OF LIFE

by Obsidian
Lyrics and Melody: Terry Knight
Music: Drums: Joey Campo, Guitar: Wil Stazeski, Bass: John Lukas

VERSE 1:
There is a Book of Life where,
Everyone is found.
Blank pages written in a
Book that is not bound.
So far removed from choices made and rectified,
Rewrite the pages in time to be retried.

CHORUS 1:
Broken hearts, shattered parts,
Wasn't that way from the start.
Wisdom of the ages, from the sages
All inside the Book of Life.

VERSE 2:
Hold on to what you know is
Truth within your heart.
The scripture guides you
And you, must do your part.
The signs are all around you, open up your eyes,
See the messages and wake up your mind.

CHORUS 2:
Broken hearts, shattered parts
Wasn't that way from the start.
Wisdom of the ages, from the sages
All inside the Book of Life, the Book of Life.

guitar solo

CHORUS 3:
Broken hearts, shattered parts
Wasn't that way from the start.
Wisdom of the ages, from the sages
All inside the Book of Life, the Book of Life.

Obsidian

Will Stazeski, Joey Campo, Terry Knight and John Lukas

"It has been a pleasure getting to know Cathy. She is a multi-talented person, great author and friend."

-- Spencer Drate

Spencer Drate (Drate / Salavetz) is a award-winning and legendary album designer. GRAMMY and National Design Award nominated and his album design in MoMA,AIGA and The Rock & Roll Hall of Fame archival collections. Authored 21 major pop-culture books. Radio and NEW HD Personality.

I can't finish this book without mentioning my friend John "Tigman" he has been part of many of our lives at The Chance and on the radio at WPDH...Doug and I spent many nights listening to Tig playing our favorites especially Pink Floyd...every radio station needs a "Tigman"

Tigman

Hey! I'm Tig. I come from the Poughkeepsie area, right here in the Hudson Valley. I'm a rocker whose favorite bands include Guns n Roses, Van Halen, Buckcherry, AC/DC, Alice in Chains, Metallica, and I love 80's hair metal. In my free time, I like to go to the rock shows and knock a few cold beers back at the local bars. I started at the Home of Rock n Roll 101.5 WPDH nearly 25 years ago.

SQUINDO

Lowbrow Illustrator and fine artist from the north-east whose freelance work ranges from numerous rock legends including Metallica, The Misfits, Ramones and Paul McCartney to professional ski and skateboard design. His fine art is primarily stain on wood panels or sculpting and is hung in galleries across the US and Europe and has been published in several books and magazines worldwide.

www.squindo.net

About the Author

Catherine Nadal's gifts of spirit communication have been with her since she was a child. She is a retired Colonel who served in the United States Army Reserve for thirty years, and she has been working as a registered nurse for more than thirty years. She is now an ordained minister in Our Lord and Lady of the Trinacrian Church in Salem, Massachusetts. Catherine is a psychic, medium, and clairvoyant. She has trained at the Arthur Findlay College in Stansted, England and has studied with Suzane Northrop and James Van Praagh in psychic workshops at Omega Institute. She has international and well-known clients in the music and entertainment business. Catherine was certified as a Forever Family Foundation Medium in 2013.

Throughout the years, Catherine has been involved with paranormal investigations of historical buildings, including the Chance Theater in Poughkeepsie, New York; The Iron Island Museum in Buffalo, New York; The Lizzie Borden House in Fall River, Massachusetts; and The Merchant's House Museum in New York City. She is devoted to helping wounded combat veterans through motorcycle charities and fundraising, especially United States Marine Corps Scout Sniper, Sergeant Eddie Ryan of Lake George, New York. Sergeant Ryan was severely wounded in Iraq on April 13, 2005. Catherine, who was stationed in a different area of Iraq at the time, has made it her business to ensure, Sergeant Ryan's heroism is never forgotten.

Catherine is avid animal lover—especially cats—and is also the author of *Seeing More Than Clouds in Your Coffee.*

Printed in the United States
by Baker & Taylor Publisher Services